WITHDRAWN

Date Due

LAUGHTER
IN THE BIBLE

GARY WEBSTER, pseud.

Gannison, Webb

LAUGHTER
IN THE BIBLE

THE BETHANY PRESS • ST. LOUIS, MO.

To
my Mother
whose laughter is gentle
and
whose love for the Bible is very deep

CONTENTS

INTRODUCTION

This book was conceived more than ten years before actual writing began. At intervals, I mentioned the project to friends. Usually the response was surprise.

"That's no subject for a book," one minister protested. "The Bible is solemn and sacred; we do not read it in order to be entertained."

His reaction, which is common, reflected the notion that laughter is chiefly linked with entertainment. To the degree that this is true, it is a modern development. Until the rise of such media of communication as printing, radio, and television, commercialized laughter was limited to the theater.

Certainly, the Bible bears no resemblance to a joke book. There are only a few passages clearly designed to cause readers to laugh. But there is deep and pervasive concern with laughter as a complex and very important human activity.

Taking into account the many varieties of laughter, there are more than 250 biblical references to it. They are most heavily concentrated in "wisdom literature": Job, Psalms, Proverbs, and Ecclesiastes. Isaiah and Jeremiah make many allusions to laughter, and the topic is of great significance to gospel writers.

9

Few books of the Bible completely ignore laughter. Short as it is, Esther includes several references to laughter, and Genesis reports some of the most vivid and illuminating case histories in all literature.

One reason we overlook so fundamental a biblical emphasis is our tendency to equate laughter with humor. Actually, many varieties of laughter comprise an elaborate spectrum with many hues and shades: amusement, mirth, delight, satire, sarcasm, wit, scorn, irony, joy, and the like.

Whatever its type, laughter is seldom pure and unqualified. For the states associated with it may be accompanied by moods of opposite type.

From time to time, we run the gamut and participate in such varied acts as:

spontaneous laughter of amusement in a life situation
polite laughter in a contrived, artificial situation
laughter of relief and relaxation
laughing with our faces but not our minds
joining in a group laugh, though we didn't hear the joke
deliberately making fun of an opponent.

No matter what the particular emphasis of an act of laughter, it comes partly as an effect of outside influences. We cannot engage in true laughter at will, though we can make the noises and facial grimaces that accompany laughter.

Neither do we laugh alone. This is a strictly social activity. You may become amused in isolation, and occasionally may even break into a chuckle; but you reserve full vocal laughter for social situations. In cases where no other persons are physically present, they are likely to be present to the imagination—made vivid by a book, magazine, letter, radio or television program.

There is one exception to this principle. A person so radically individual that he is incommunicado—not functionally social—may laugh with great fervor in total isolation. Society uses such labels as "psychosis" and "insanity" to indicate such personality states. Whether it be Hamlet's disturbed laughter on the stage or the strained giggling of a schizophrenic next door, sounds of this sort frighten rather than amuse.

These factors give some clues to reasons for laughter's prominence in Scripture. Because the Bible is a book that comes out of life and is directed to life, nothing that is human is alien to it.

We shall not find it easy to analyze biblical treatment of this theme, or, indeed, to make a neat dissection of individual specimens. On the contrary, the more we examine the nature and varieties of laughter, the more profoundly we shall be impressed with its complexities.

Part of the difficulty lies in the fact that laughter is not a self-contained entity. Always, it is an aspect of a larger situation that includes it as one component. To sever laughter from its context is like cutting a blossom from a flower. It is difficult to study the flower as one constituent of an elaborate living system that includes it. But it would be futile to reach conclusions based on familiarity with morning glory blossoms, studied without regard for morning glory vines, soil, water, air, and climate.

Just so, laughter must be considered as one phase of a complex system. In no case is an event laughable from all perspectives. One participant in a practical joke may laugh so hard he has to gasp for breath—but another will burn with indignation. That is, laughter always has both social and individual dimensions.

So viewed, laughter is recognized as one aspect of the paradox by which you and I can become fully human only by entering the double door of individual plus group life. Because laughter is oriented toward man as an individual in isolation as well as toward man as a social being, it serves as a mirror to show us things about ourselves we would not otherwise see.

Therefore it is not strange that laughter should have been pondered by profound thinkers outside the Bible as well as in it. Its nature and significance occupied major philosophers of classical times. Indeed, since the time of Aristotle, man himself has been defined as "a rational animal capable of laughter."

Thomas Hobbes gave a fresh twist to classical ideas by suggesting that laughter is related to the biological struggle. We laugh, he said, because "sudden glory" stems from seeing our competitors stumble and fall. More recently, Anthony M. Ludovici supported the same basic notion by describing laughter as man's way of showing his fangs.

Henri Bergson became intrigued with laughter prior to 1884, pondered its meaning for sixteen years before writing his famous essay on the subject. Like those of ancient thinkers, his analysis is suggestive but by no means definitive.

Man's special place in the scheme of things has been variously indicated by defining him as the thinking, tool-making, social, speaking, worshiping, and laughing animal. Wylie Sopher, noting the range of these attempts to indicate human distinctiveness, suggests that the final label is the most enigmatic of all because we know neither what laughter is, nor what causes us to laugh.

Make no mistake about it, therefore. Laughter in general —and laughter in the Bible in particular—is no light subject. It bears on fundamental issues of life and thought.

Some months ago the making of a typographical error led to the sudden insight that there is but one letter's difference between the *cosmic* and the *comic*. Add something to the comic, and it becomes cosmic in significance; take a bit from the cosmic and it becomes comic!

Chesterton dubbed our subject "the beautiful madness called laughter." Part of its appeal centers in the fact that while the most erudite scholars do not understand it, the simplest of men can participate in it.

All of us do, in fact, laugh frequently and in a great variety of ways. Through the lens of scripture, a survey of this sublimely mysterious activity will throw light on life as a whole.

1

MAJOR MOTIFS
IN THE OLD TESTAMENT

Even a quick sampling of biblical allusions shows that Israel's people placed a premium on laughter and states of joy associated with it.

Guests expected, as a matter of course, that hosts would so entertain them that both could laugh. When Jacob slipped away from Laban before this social ritual could be completed, the older man felt himself injured. "Why did you flee secretly, and cheat me, and did not tell me," he demanded, "so that I might have sent you away with mirth and songs, with tambourine and lyre?" (Genesis 31:27)

Laughter was associated with prosperity and contentment, so provision of resources with which to engage in it

15

was a mark of special favor. Joseph sent food from his own table to each of his brothers, but Benjamin's portion was five times that of the rest. Spontaneously and naturally, therefore, they joined the favored youth, "drank and were merry with him" (Genesis 43:34).

Inspired by the word of the Lord, Zechariah saw a vision of the new Jerusalem. One symbol of bliss in the redeemed society is the pervasive gaiety of a city "full of boys and girls playing in its streets" (Zech. 8:5). Jeremiah used different images to express the same idea. Through him, God promises that in the rebuilt city, joyous folk will live in the palace and all the dwellings;

> "Out of them shall come songs of thanksgiving,
> and the voices of those who make merry."
>
> —Jeremiah 30:19

Consciousness of having been ransomed gives men radiant faces. Maidens will express their joy through dancing, while young men and old will make merry.

> "Again you shall adorn yourself with timbrels,
> and shall go forth in the dance of the merrymakers."
>
> —Jeremiah 31:4

Such pictures of the day of the Lord go far to make religion joyful rather than sombre. Heaven, whatever its place and state, will be marked by exuberant happiness.

Given so high an appraisal of laughter, it follows that humiliation comes from being the butt of jeers. He who laughs because of God's bounty feels himself punished when he is ridiculed.

Sent to judge sinful Jerusalem, Ezekial concluded that her idolatry caused God to make the city "a reproach to the nations, and a mocking to all the countries. Those who

16

are near and those who are far from you will mock you."
(Ezekial 22:4). Having played the harlot with other nations by paying homage to their idols,

"you shall be laughed at and held in derision."—Ezekial 23:32.

Much the same verdict is implied in those condemnations that emphasize lack of capacity to make merry. In the case of those who have stirred the wrath of God,

The mirth of the timbrels is stilled,
   the noise of the jubilant has ceased.
   the mirth of the lyre is stilled.

—Isaiah 24:8

Sorrow is the dominant mood among the once-victorious but now overwhelmed ones, turned rebels, for whom therefore

There is an outcry in the streets for lack of wine;
   all joy has reached its eventide;
   the gladness of the earth is banished.

—Isaiah 24:11

Such absence of laughter is not accidental. Neither is it incidental, to be taken as a matter of course. Rather, it is a potent sign of divine judgment. God deliberately establishes such conditions that erring ones cannot achieve joy. "I will make to cease from the cities of Judah and from the streets of Jerusalem the voice of mirth and the voice of gladness," God threatens again and again. (Jeremiah 7:34, 16:9, 25:10)

Among the more sensitive of Israel's seekers, such warnings are underscored by recognition that past woes were sent by God. It is not enough to blame poor military leaders or lack of national preparedness. Providence is at work in

17

those instances when nations laugh at God's chosen ones, derelict in their obedience. Assyrians and Babylonians are but instruments to accomplish the divine will;

> Thou hast made us the taunt of our neighbors,
> the derision and scorn of those about us.
>
> —Psalm 44:13

Laughter, then, was serious business in Old Testament times. Men perhaps valued it in a fashion somewhat like that in which some modern Americans value prosperity and peace of mind. At least a rough index to a man's status in God's eyes could be found by observing whether he laughed or was laughed at, and how hard. Modified in relation to a wide variety of specific situations, these fundamental motifs bear upon many biblical references to laughter.

Always, however, smiles and chuckles were linked with everyday activities. Amusements practiced for the sake of amusement left little imprint upon scripture.

Yet there are distinct and significant clues to special kinds of laughter that were evoked by playing with words. Riddles and enigmas, plus ancient equivalents of the pun and the *double entendre*, were prominent in Hebrew life and thought.

Word play gained prominence with sages and prophets partly because it is a basic source of humor among all peoples. But in the case of the ancient Hebrews, more was involved. In a fashion hard for us to grasp from the perspective of a culture in which words are mechanically spewed out en masse, many early thinkers regarded spoken sounds and written shapes as having innate potency. At times, veneration was such that words were regarded as semidivine—endowed with fearful capacity for good and evil.

It is this point of view that is reflected in Genesis, chapter 1, where God's spoken word is the active agent in creation. On a lower plane and to a lesser degree, Adam and Eve share in the work of creation by giving names to all the beasts. Until a thing has been named—has had a word attached to it as a handle by which to grasp it and pass it from mind to mind—it is not an object of discussion or investigation.

Words, therefore, are potent agents. Far from passive, they have capacity to stir minds of men in such fashion that creative discovery takes place.

Meanings attach to words in dynamic rather than static fashion. When first invented or coined, a word may have but one meaning. By the time it has been in use long enough to enter general speech, it is certain to have several recognized meanings. That connotation which is "right" in a given instance is determined not by the word alone, but by the total situation. Consequently, it is a universal experience to discover that a word shows two or more meanings within a single unit of discourse.

Deliberate exploitation of verbal plasticity underlies many forms of humor. It is basic to both the pun and the riddle. While both may be employed in modern life purely for the sake of a laugh, near-sacredness of words in Hebrew thought made word play solemn as well as amusing.

Guests invited to Samson's wedding feast were challenged by a riddle. Their inability to solve it made them the target of Samson's laughter; they were defeated in an intellectual struggle. Seriousness of the matter is indicated by Delilah's reaction. Her husband, she said, could not possibly love her because he gave the wrong answer in response to her pleading (Judges 16:10, 15). Personally as well as in sympathy with her countrymen, she resented the triumphant laughter of her bridegroom.

19

Verbal contests may have been standard features of marriage celebrations and other periods of merrymaking. Solomon's fame brought the Queen of Sheba to his court for the express purpose of testing him with hard questions (1 Kings 10:1). An ancient manuscript, published early in this century, preserves nineteen riddles that tradition ascribes to the dusky queen. One of them runs: "Without moving while living, it moves when its head is cut off." Solomon got that one instantly: "A tree, made into a ship!"

Propounding of riddles is still a host-guest pastime in numerous cultures. Talmudic lore preserves many ancient specimens of such parlor jousting. A long-time favorite was: "What animal has one voice living, and seven voices dead?" Only the initiated knew the answer: "The ibis— from whose carcass seven different musical instruments are made."

Though entertainment features were prominent in such verbal contests, they did not eliminate strong elements of seriousness. In a sense, one challenged by a riddle was invited to play a game that was intended to provide amusement, but involved grave consequences. Something of the same spirit marks such modern contests as college football games, in which both players and spectators seek a good time but are grim far more often than amused.

In both Brittany and the Celebes, riddles remained popular until recent centuries—but custom forbade asking them except when there was a corpse in the village. Turkish tribesmen of Central Asia long preserved a ritual by which girls publicly propounded riddles to their suitors—who were punished if unable to give the answers.

Sometimes the seriousness of such a contest so dominated a situation that laughter was absent. That was the case with the enigma hurled at King Belshazzar. Confronted by

20

mysterious words on the wall, he was not amused. Rather, "the king's color changed and his thoughts alarmed him; his limbs gave way, and his knees knocked together." (Daniel 5:6)

Enchanters, Chaldeans, and astrologers were brought to solve the riddle—i.e., give the king victory over the challenge of the unknown. Their failure led to Daniel's opportunity. He was consulted because of his reputation for skill in interpreting dreams and explaining riddles.

True to his reputation, the Hebrew found an interpretation. It turned on the fact that each mysterious word, *mene, tekel,* and *parsin,* had two distinct sets of meanings. Discarding the obvious meaning as the name for an act of weighing or measuring, Daniel made spiritual applications and warned that God has *numbered* the days, *weighed* men and found them lacking, and *divided* the kingdom. In spite of the ominous import of that solution, the king was so delighted that he heaped rewards upon the man whose wit overcame the mystery of words.

Part of the pleasure that stems from solving a riddle is due to the fact that the answer is not a fruit of striving or of logical analysis. It comes suddenly, even abruptly, and usually conveys a sense of having been given rather than achieved. Such sudden finding of an answer is a major element in all forms of explosive laughter; to "get the point" of a joke as a result of laborious explanation is no pathway to laughter.

To Israel's seekers for wisdom, riddles were much more than stimuli to sudden discovery erupting in laughter. Both scholarly investigation and teaching of disciples by a master were aided by use of riddles. Solomon's proverbs were framed to instruct both the simple and the wise, so that men might gain skill

21

to understand a proverb and a figure,
the words of the wise and their riddles.

—Proverbs 1:6

Such a view of the riddle, seldom held in modern life, is witnessed by a speech fossil which makes "the riddle of the universe" a deadly serious matter.

More than one philosopher has wondered why twentieth-century children get great pleasure from riddles at some stages of their development, while few adults enjoy them. No final answers can be given. But at least two factors probably affect this situation. Adults are likely to be so skillful in use of words that answers are obvious. This eliminates the mental leap across the spark gap, essential to sudden understanding and consequent triumphant laughter. At the same time, typical answers are likely to be too far-fetched, not sufficiently coherent by adult standards. As a source of intellectual striving and joyful delight of solution, the riddle therefore plays an insignificant part in modern thought.

That is not the case with word play of more sophisticated types. Verbal elements are prominent in nearly all humor; even cartoons usually require explanatory words. Many rib-ticklers are wholly verbal, turning upon sudden recognition of a relationship between two sets of meaning.

Considerable skill is required to understand quips that exploit regional dialects, so there is corresponding heartiness in the laughter of understanding Feature writers get warm reactions from use of such material as "definitions from the Charleston, S. C., dictionary." Even persons who have never struggled to understand warmly soft Charlestonese may enjoy solving the riddle of what mock versions of the sounds mean.

Here are samples from the column written by Ashley Cooper in the Charleston *News and Courier*: "Abode—wooden plank; A Boot—approximately; Braid—what you make to-est from, to go along with beckon and a-igs for brake-fuss; Flow—what you stand on in a house; Ice Cool—institution of learning."

Columnist Earl Wilson has responded in kind by suggesting a few samples of New Yorkese, whose definitions include: "Fit—strollin' down Fit Ammenyou; Career—the country next to Japan; Lexicon—the avenue parallel with Medicine Avenue; Wading—like in wading room of a doctor's office."

Formal epigrams are only one step removed from such juggling of words and playing with sounds and meanings. Usually limited to a single sentence, the epigram often rests upon exploitation of one or more terms with widely divergent connotations. That reader who "gets the point" receives a whiplash surge of meaning, delights in doing so, and smiles or chuckles at such contrived patterns as these:

The only thing a modern girl knows about cooking is how to bring a husband to boil.

Wisdom is that fine line of distinction which lies between keeping your chin up and sticking your chin out.

Much word play erupts spontaneously, without conscious purpose. Four receptionists or secretaries walked into the coffee shop of an Indianapolis medical arts building.

"Are you gonna have coffee again this morning?" the leader inquired.

"No. Make mine tea."

"Sounds good. I think I'll have tea, too."

Behind them, the third member of the group broke into vocal experiments—not particularly talking to anyone and probably oblivious of others in the room. Had she been conscious of an audience, she probably would have been overwhelming with embarrassment at realizing she half chanted, half said:

" 'Tea, too,' eh? Tea, three. Tea, four. Let's have a tea party. I'll tee off . . . "

All but meaningless, such spontaneous toying with sounds and symbols is now more characteristic of children than adults. It occurs most often within the intimacy of the family.

Many biblical examples of the *double entendre* have so lost their significance that, for us, they scarcely constitute specimens of wit. Whether early listeners and readers reacted to them by laughing, it is impossible to know. But it is certain that potential for laughter exists in verbal patterns that convey serious ideas through puns and riddles.

One of Jeremiah's earliest oracles rests on verbal factors, though they do not emerge in translation. Asked by the Lord what he saw, he replied: " 'I see a rod of almond.' " This brought divine commendation: " 'You have seen well, for I am watching over my word to perform it.' " (Jeremiah 1:11-12) In Hebrew, words for *almond* and *watching* are identical except for vowel points; their use therefore invites first bewilderment and then delighted understanding. Similar juggling of words is exhibited in Amos 8:1-2, where a word is first pointed to mean "summer fruit" and then repeated with points changing the meaning to "end."

Some passages that were originally in riddle form have been edited so they appear as statements of fact rather than questions. At the same time, much word play that was prominent in the original has disappeared in translation. Therefore we can only surmise that chuckles from solving a riddle long greeted such a formula as that of Proverbs 30:15-16:

> Three things are never satisfied;
>> four never say, "Enough":
> Sheol, the barren womb,
>> the earth ever thirsty for water,
>> and the fire which never says, "Enough."

Linguistic and cultural variables have blinded us to factors that made many early stories humorous when recited by tribal elders as young men sat about camp fires listening. At least four such cases can be distinguished in Genesis alone. Because their emphases bear upon reappraisal of systems of value, these tales are discussed in Chapter 10.

Recognizing that time and change have erected barriers so that we can never plumb the depths of Old Testament laughter, we cannot escape recognition of its prominent place in life and thought. Whatever else it may be, the heritage of Israel is not somber. Abraham's descendants valued laughter so highly that they regarded it as an index to divine approval or condemnation, and deliberately employed words to evoke both laughter and new meanings.

2

TOKEN OF THE DIVINE IMPRINT

Centuries before Moses led his people from the land of pyramid and sphinx, Greek philosophers told their own legend of the sphinx. According to it, this creature had the body of a lion, wings of a bird, tail of a serpent, and head of a woman.

She lived in a cavern near Thebes, and commanded the highway leading to the city. Every traveler was challenged with a riddle: What animal walks on four legs in the morning, two at noon, and three in the evening?

Multitudes proved unable to solve the riddle, so were killed and eaten by the sphinx. One day the hero Oedipus came to Thebes, and was confronted with the enigma. He declared the animal in question to be man—who crawls on hands and feet as an infant, walks on two feet during maturity, and relies upon a staff in old age.

Enraged at suffering so stunning an intellectual defeat, the sphinx howled with rage. Then she jumped from the cliff and was killed.

Hebrew riddles, in common with that of the sphinx, often made answers serious business. Laughter belonged only to the victor in the struggle of wits. Defeated parties forfeited prestige if not life itself, for tragedy was blended with comedy somewhat like seriousness with play in a bowling match.

It was not accidental that the riddle of the sphinx should revolve about the creature *man*. For man is the only organism on earth who has capacity to pose riddles or laugh upon solving them. Men laugh for many reasons and at a great variety of things. All normal persons laugh at something; no other creature laughs at anything. There are hundreds of thousands of species on our planet; only one has capacity to tell or understand a joke.

Domesticated chimpanzees, tickled about the neck, sometimes respond with sounds that have some qualities of laughter. And the gibbon "giggles" in rather musical fashion. But even so liberal a thinker as the social psychologist McDougall hesitates to use "laughter" as a label for such patterns of behavior.

Numerous analysts have called attention to the fact that a context entirely lacking in human qualities cannot be comical. Monkeys get more laughs than any other animals at the zoo precisely because they excel in ability to imitate mankind. Notice the significant fact that they imitate rather than duplicate. Exact duplication would reduce the animal's power to stir laughter. It is the "almost human," simultaneously seen as manlike and yet wholly nonhuman, that makes monkeys the clowns of the zoo.

In *Life Is Worth Living,* Fulton J. Sheen suggests that man's capacity to break into a laugh is itself symbolic. It points to the fact that there is a radical break in the stream of life, with man high above every other creature. Part of this difference, he says in a happy phrase, is reflected by the fact that "Man is the only joker in the deck of nature."

Conveyed through the vehicle of a dramatic story rather than scientific analysis, that is precisely the message of Scripture. Neither in the Old Testament nor the New do we get away from the fundamental truth conveyed in God's decision: " 'Let us make man in our image, after our likeness; and let them have dominion over the fish of the sea, and over the birds of the air, and over the cattle, and over all the earth, and over every creeping thing that creeps upon the earth.' " (Genesis 1:26)

Without exhausting the significance of man's uniqueness, laughter is an index to its reality. That this is no minor matter is indicated by the world-famous men who have dealt with it. Both Plato and Augustine emphasized its significance. So did Francis Bacon, Friedrich Nietzsche, and Arthur Schopenhauer.

The problem of laughter as a distinctively human activity was formally discussed in Rome during the second century, under the leadership of Porphyry of Tyre. Yet it was still significant when Julian Huxley wrote his noted *Man in the Modern World.*

Dante called the most famous literary work of a thousand years *The Divine Comedy.* John Milton puzzled over why men laugh. So did Lord Byron and Thomas Hobbes. It occupied the minds of Herbert Spencer, Charles Darwin, and Sigmund Freud. Immanuel Kant attempted to analyze laughter, as did the great contemporary interpreter of language and meaning, Ernst Cassirer.

Though differing widely in their views concerning specific aspects of laughter, these and other thinkers agreed on a vital point: laughter is practiced by man alone. Nietzsche suggested a partial explanation: "Man alone," he said, "suffers so excruciatingly in the world that he was compelled to invent laughter." Jean Paul Richter spent years analyzing collected definitions of the comic. In the end, he solemnly concluded that their one common quality is that they themselves are comical.

This paradox is central to one of the longest and most difficult biblical passages dealing with laughter. Virtually the entire Book of Ecclesiastes bears upon this matter. While the vocabulary of laughter is not widely used, the message of the Preacher rests upon a philosophy of laughter and of tears. His conclusion, itself a subtle bit of word play, underscores the double orientation of every event we brand as humorous: "I said of laughter, 'It is mad.' " (Ecclesiastes 2:2)

Out of all this inquiry into the nature and meaning of a reaction shown only by the creature made in the image of God, one emphasis is clear. Though laughter is far from understood, its development in man is linked with his capacity to use symbols—to engage in communication of abstract ideas by means of a man-shaped set of artificial pointers, which we call "words." For whatever else it may be, laughter is an aspect of communication. It is therefore restricted to the social life of creatures who exchange ideas, as opposed to gestures and signals exchanged among non-humans.

Though he is unique in capacity to laugh, man is not alone in his enjoyment of play. There is no doubt that a kitten can have a hilarious time chasing its own tail. But after centuries of domestication and exposure to words, the animal is totally deficient in ability to understand a riddle or a funny story—whether its subject be cat-kind or mankind.

How humans gain capacity to laugh is an enigma quite as obscure as laughter itself. This much is established: until a newborn individual becomes a social creature instead of a solitary one, he does not take part in true laughter.

As early as the first century, Pliny the Elder suggested that ability to laugh does not develop before the fortieth day of life. Charles Darwin tickled the feet of his children, and charted their reactions. He saw what he regarded as the first real smile at 45 days, and the first genuine laugh at about 100 days.

Since 1875 social psychologists have given much attention to both laughter and smiling. Babies, watched from infancy, have given some clues to each. But bubbling and giggling in response to tickling or jostling, even though it produces smiles and the sounds of laughter, is not identical with amusement at a joke.

In the case of maturing individuals, true laughter is nearly always associated with use of symbols and abstract ideas. This is especially obvious in the case of verbal humor, which rests upon symbols completely divorced from a physical situation such as cat-chasing-tail-for-fun or baby-giggling-from-tickling. Take, for example, this jingle with which farm folk twit their city cousins:

> There was a wise guy from the city
> Who met what he thought was a kitty.
>   He gave it a pat,
>   Saying "What a nice cat!"
> They buried his clothes, out of pity.

Notice that there can be no laughter in the case of those persons incapable of handling symbols, or unacquainted with their several sets of meanings. Some level of acquaintance with kittens and skunks is basic to understanding; understanding is preliminary to laughter.

Laughter is a hallmark of man because only humans have God-given capacity for abstract thought and for communication through symbols. No matter how skillful the spider in weaving her web or the termite in cutting its tunnels, these creatures are forever barred from understanding a profound saying from Ecclesiastes, a clever quip by Bennett Cerf, or a yarn about an encounter between a preacher and a platter of fried chicken.

For men and men alone, there is inevitably and inescapably "a time to weep, and a time to laugh" (Ecclesiastes 3:4).

But this is a matter of utmost gravity, for part of the meaning of one's life is hinted in his laughing and his weeping. Without using the language of Scripture, William Hazlitt came very close to the biblical view when he suggested that "Man is the only animal that laughs and weeps; for he is the only animal that is struck with the difference between what things are, and what they ought to be." That is, alone among creatures, man has capacity to recognize the radical break between the ideal and the actual. He not only responds to this tension because he is equipped with what we call a conscience; his response is a significant index to his goals and values.

As preserved in Luke's Gospel, the Savior's list of blessings and woes comes to sharp focus. It serves as a set of standards by which to distinguish between true disciples and worldly minded camp followers. Doubly emphasized, these standards include due attention to the gravity of laughter and the import of tears: " 'Blessed are you that weep now, for you shall laugh.' " (Luke 6:21)

31

In the first century as now, sin and misery abounded. Men become absorbed with material things and lose sight of eternal values. Weeds of selfishness, lust and pride choke the crops of individual lives and threaten to spread over the fields of whole cultures. A few sensitive seekers for God survey themselves and their fellows, then weep over what they see. Some persons in every age and most in many ages laugh with delight at the same spectacle.

That is one reason Jesus lifted up the significance of laughter as a clue to man's spiritual condition. That future joy which he listed as belonging to those who now weep will not come as a "reward." Rather, it is an inevitable consequence of a way of life. Only those made sad by the dilemma of sin and lostness are capable of delight at the nonmaterial glory of God's future kingdom.

We are not so much judged by God as by ourselves. Tears shed by Jesus' followers are not for sufferings or hardships. Rather, they flow because the pure of heart are troubled by evils resulting from man's turning away from the highest he knows. Surveying the same human situation through less sensitive eyes, many howl with laughter.

Hans Christian Andersen once told a story of a proud emperor. Tricksters wheedled him into appearing in public stark naked. There is indeed a ludicrous element in thinking of an oriental monarch, splendid in all his uncovered wrinkles and bulges, trying to preside over his court.

If laughter stems from thinking of an emperor who has no robes, tears should result from pondering the paradox of fine garments which have no man. All the outward appearances are observed, but where a child of God should be found, there is emptiness.

Only one who has glimpsed something of the vision of the Preacher and sees both tragedy and humor in the fact that "All is vanity" (Ecclesiastes 1:2) has eyes sufficiently

32

keen to distinguish between a man who has no clothes and clothes which have no man.

There is a famous spiritual whose burden is a plaintive lament over failure to recognize the fact that the infant Jesus was the long-sought Savior. "Sweet little Jesus boy," runs the haunting confession, "we wouldn't have treated you so, if we'd known who you was. . . ."

That is precisely the problem.

A Pharisee, holy by all the conventional standards of his era, glances casually at a man-child lying in a manger. He sees only another peasant's son, another mouth to feed. A horny-handed shepherd, given a special viewpoint by listening to the songs of angels, tiptoes into a stable to discover the very Word made flesh.

To many, the crucifixion was an occasion for a holiday. It was an invitation to jest at the pretensions of a carpenter's son who had tried to lead men on a new way. Every fresh brutality of the soldiers was an occasion for a burst of laughter. "See, he cried for water, and that gay dog of a Roman is giving him vinegar! What a laugh! This is the country fellow who thought he could tell us how to behave in Jerusalem!"

If this line of thought appears bizarre, consider for a moment the last animated cartoon you saw at the movies. Perhaps it dealt with the misadventures of a cat or the utterly brutal triumph of a crow over a fox. Viewers who see cat or fox as an antagonist are likely to howl with delight at each new piece of brutality.

A movie version of the World War I experiences of Sergeant Alvin York reached a moment of great tension when Germans seemed at the point of victory. York's sudden and dramatic attack, in which he cut down whole pockets of Germans with a machine gun, produced explosive bursts of laughter from many groups of viewers.

For the moment, they were incapable of really seeing bullets, blood, and sudden death.

" 'Woe to you that laugh now, for you shall mourn and weep.' " (Luke 6:25)

Jesus' terse summary suggests that the kingdom of God will be denied those who fail to gain sufficient sensitivity to see the reality of evil and to weep over it.

Many generations earlier, Ezekiel was given insight by God. In his agony of striving for yet deeper understanding, he came to recognize that God sends messengers to a city or nation in order to " 'put a mark upon the foreheads of the men who sigh and groan over all the abominations that are committed in it.' " (Ezekiel 9:4) It is these marked men—those who weep when others laugh—who will be spared from the divine wrath.

Laughter, then, is far more than merriment. Just as it is a sign that distinguishes the being made "a little lower than God," so it is a rod to measure him. In somewhat the same way that laughter sets men apart from beasts, one man's chuckles set him apart from another. Laughter provides at least a general index to one's cultural background, range of experiences, and basic loyalties.

Many laugh at human failure, thereby show themselves far from the kingdom. Others are so keenly distressed by the human dilemma that they seek divine rescue and through it inherit eternal joy. Perhaps it will not strain a famous maxim too severely to paraphrase it:

"Tell me what you find amusing, and I will tell you what you are."

3

THEY WHO LAUGH ALIKE,
BEGIN TO THINK ALIKE

Laughter's role as a basic social force is easier to recognize than to analyze. Any example of laughter, however simple, can be a starting point for searching questions about group processes and their meaning.

Stepping on an express elevator in a Boston department store, a customer noticed three men ahead of him. Two other men and a woman followed him as the elevator operator called in mechanical fashion: "Lunchroom only, please. This car stops at the sixth floor, only."

One man quickly pushed his way out and turned to another car. As the operator shut the door, her feminine passenger turned and inquired: "Could you let me off on five?"

Shaking her head and already pulling the handle that would halt the elevator on six, the operator apologized. "I'm sorry, madam. You'll have to take another car down to five. On your left, please . . ."

Other passengers having stepped away, the curious one turned to the operator. "I suppose you have something like this happen several times a week, eh? They just don't read the signs, do they?"

She broke into a broad smile, positively chortled in reply: "It's a lot more often than several times a week! I hardly ever take up a car without having somebody on it by mistake—in spite of two big signs and my announcement!"

Laughter of that elevator operator is interesting partly because of its timing. All the way up to the sixth floor, she recognized that one passenger was aboard by mistake. But she did not so much as smile until conversation led to shared recognition of that mistake. That is, her laughter had a social dimension.

In your own recent experience can you think of instances in which you laughed aloud without having someone to echo your chuckles? When you are the only member of a group who shows amusement, do others ask why you are laughing?

Henri Bergson declared that it is all but impossible to respond to the comical in isolation. Emerson expressed the same idea. "Why has my motley diary no jokes?" he asked himself, and replied, "Because it is a soliloquy, and every man is grave alone."

It is one thing to recognize that real laughter has social dimensions; it is another thing to survey effects of group hilarity upon individuals who make up a group. Perhaps the most vivid of biblical cases is that of Philistine rejoicing at the woes of Samson.

36

That mighty maker of jokes and riddles saw laughter from only one point of view so long as he swaggered and blustered about the land. Captured and blinded, he was put to slave labor. While the once-gay Hebrew strained at the machine that ground their grain, Philistines prepared for a festival in honor of their god, Dagon.

At last the great day arrived. Philistines streamed into their mighty temple, pushed and squeezed until it would hold no more. Latecomers climbed on the roof until it sagged with the weight of 3,000 eager spectators.

Preliminaries dragged on—almost endlessly, it seemed. Impatient ones clapped, cheered, and stamped their feet. Excitement mounted with hilarity. "And when their hearts were merry, they said, 'Call Samson, that he may make sport for us.'" (Judges 16:25)

Nothing evokes greater hilarity than a festival at which some captured Samson is exhibited. In order to make the crowd laugh, the captive must be an enemy. He must represent a challenge to established customs, values, or ideas. To the degree that he threatens to overthrow some Dagon, his public squirmings delight all Dagon's followers.

Long after it fell as a prey to its enemies, Prohibition remained a sure-fire subject with which to provoke roars from the crowd. Chastity, fidelity, and sobriety often evoke mirth when humiliated in public.

Samson's tormenters did not call for him at once. They knew he would be exhibited—he was the attraction that drew the crowd. But individual Philistines still thought of him with awe. Taken one by one, probably most or all the fighting men at the festival feared him.

That fear was lost, however, when men and women surrendered part of their individuality by becoming active members of the crowd. Gradually a kind of group frenzy developed.

37

At length some rash fellow, made brave by boasting, called for Samson. "Yes, bring out Samson!" echoed a neighbor.

"Samson, Samson! We want Samson!"

Rolling through the tightly packed audience and gathering momentum as it went, the chant became an imperious demand. Now no man feared the captive. Caution was thrown to the winds. Samson must sport for his foes.

Though the direction of its impact may vary widely, group influence always bends individuals toward conformity. It is no accident that we laugh most heartily when caught up in the spirit of a merry group. From tears to anger, all emotional reactions are magnified and intensified as individuals communicate their feelings to one another.

That is one basis for our desire to come together. From public entertainment to corporate worship, group activity tends to lift us out of ourselves. Part but not all of this effect may be transmitted by radio and television. No matter what the skill of photographers and announcers, a football game viewed at home lacks the strange dynamic that comes from watching it as a member of a yelling, groaning crowd.

Rightly used, these indefinable effects may constitute opportunities for religious leaders. This is obviously the case in mass evangelism. Still, the catalytic effect of laughter and other group activities is a source of danger. For like the Philistines who literally laughed themselves to death at Samson, individuals who yield to group forces are likely to modify their goals and actions in the process.

One reason speakers, playwrights, and entertainers seek to evoke laughter is that it fosters involvement by the listener. Each individual in an audience becomes a participant instead of a spectator when he laughs. He is socialized; his individuality is reduced, and personality barriers are lowered. Sometimes the process is involuntary—producing laughter that is all but meaningless in retrospect.

In a group of 60 persons, a comment from the chairman brought a general laugh. One member of the audience did not hear the quip. He turned to his neighbor at the left, who was laughing vigorously, and whispered: "What did he say?"

"I don't know," she confessed, her amusement suddenly gone. "I couldn't hear, myself. But it must have been good. . . ."

Her chuckles, hearty and genuine, were a fruit of having been drawn into the contagion of laughter as a social catalyst. Centuries ago, the Roman orator Quintilian pointed out that laughter may be tyrannical. It frequently erupts against one's will, and because its power is all but irresistible, "it often changes the tendency of the greatest affairs."

In a few minutes of fervent shouting and laughing as a crowd, men may reduce themselves to carbon copies of whatever vocal leaders hold the stage at the moment. Ridicule can be incendiary socially. "Scoffers set a city aflame," warned Israel's wise men (Proverbs 29:8). Because social conflagrations are easily kindled and spread beyond control, it is traditional to regard members of a mob as fickle. Individuality having been surrendered, responses of the group influence or determine actions of its members.

Early in his ministry, Jesus attracted huge crowds: hordes flocked to him from "Jerusalem and all Judea and all the region about the Jordan" (Matthew 3:5). These enthusiastic converts confessed their sins and were baptized. At the moment, they were in earnest. Yet some of them took up the cry when, a few months later, another crowd began to shout: "Crucify him! Crucify him!"

39

Through cultural pressure, which is a special kind of crowd influence, conditioning of the individual begins very early. Pervading social forces both push and tug, kneading every child toward uniformity in thoughts and values. To be a good boy, a youngster must hate what his elders hate, laugh at the notions the crowd considers funny. In "Carefully Taught," from *South Pacific*, Oscar Hammerstein II breaks a lance against the iron knight who tries to ride down all who insist upon being individuals instead of carbon copies of the cultural pattern:

> You've got to be taught
> Before it's too late,
> Before you are six, or seven, or eight,
> To hate all the people your relatives hate;
> You've got to be carefully taught.[1]

Much such teaching is in the form of social pressure to laugh at the right places in the drama of life.

Continued through many years, strokes with social sandpaper may cut away all the distinctive features that mark a person as distinguished from a puppet. Using humor as a bludgeon with which to attack those who cede their individuality to the group, Oscar Wilde quipped: "Most people are other people. Their thoughts are someone else's opinions, their lives a mimicry, their passions a quotation."

In a few minutes of fervent shouting and laughing as a crowd, men may reduce themselves to *ersatz* versions of whatever vocal leader holds the stage at the moment. Some effects of such yielding are trivial and transient. They may lead to nothing more significant than placing a jingle about "itty bitty fishes" at the top of the Hit Parade, or overloading stores with Davy Crockett caps.

---

[1]Copyright © 1949 by Richard Rogers and Oscar Hammerstein 2nd, Williamson Music, Inc., New York, New York, Publisher and owner of publication of allied rights.

Other effects may be more lasting—and deadly.

Take, for example, the witch mania. Sparks began flying late in the fifteenth century. Soon fires were blazing throughout western Europe. Once the masses became convinced that many ills resulted from work of demons who disguised themselves as old women, no grandmother was safe.

Almost overnight there sprang up a class of professional witch hunters. That is the case in almost every instance of social frenzy. Leaders incite mobs, who create a demand for more leaders, who whip new crowds into excitement and make places for more agitators.

A single witch hunter burned 41 poor Italian women in a single province. He was quickly put to shame by followers of the German zealot, Springer. He tortured his prisoners to secure confessions, drove them to the stake and scaffold at the rate of 500 in a year. In Geneva alone, hundreds of witches were burned in 1515-16. A single witch finder, Remigius, boasted that in fifteen years he burned 900 demons concealed in the bodies of aged peasants.

In any age, when masses shout together and laugh together so heartily that individuals surrender their sovereignty, there is danger of a catastrophe.

No one can live apart from the social order. Such a goal is not desirable, and if it were desirable would not be possible. Within limits, we need to discover the thrill of joining in great mass movements, of identifying ourselves with viewpoints of groups to which we belong. By singing, praying, weeping, and laughing together, men and women form bonds that can give new direction and purpose to each individual included in a group.

Yet every social unit, to the degree that it forms internal bonds, tears down uniqueness that contributes to the integrity of its members. Most of us find it easy to join a

41

chorus—almost any chorus—in which masses of our fellows applaud one set of ideas and ridicule another. Global war has shaken but not demolished the tendency to bow down before sovereign rightness of the crowd—almost any crowd, provided it is big enough and vocal enough.

It was repudiation of this standard that led Jeremiah to reject laughter and espouse solitude:

> I did not sit in the company of merrymakers,
>   nor did I rejoice;
> I sat alone, because thy hand was upon me.
>
> —Jeremiah 15:17

By all means, do not repudiate laughter. Laugh, and enjoy it. But be cautious about joining in any making of sport that will lead you to endorse goals and actions you would repudiate if you surveyed them in the freedom of solitude.

If God's cause is to go forward, we must have more creative individuals who dare to withdraw from the crowd and weep while others laugh. "Blessed are you when men hate you, and when they exclude you and revile you, and cast out your name as evil, on account of the Son of man!" (Luke 6:22)

4

SUPPORTER
OF THE *STATUS QUO*

Man is not only the creature who laughs. Alone among inhabitants of earth, he lives in an elaborate social order that includes communication through words, gestures, and other media. Complex nonphysical bonds hold together groups, institutions, and other components of society.

An inspired individual is the only channel through which creative thought and discovery may flow. Movement to appropriate and shape the absolutely novel takes place in solitude. Even when an inventor seizes a radical new idea in the midst of a crowd, he is solitary as a creator.

Made in the image of God the Creator, man has such potential for innovation that agents of restraint are necessary. Were there no check upon translating new ideas into action, individuals would go off at top speed in erratic fashion. Society, as an organized group of persons who conform to standards, could not exist. Over and over, disruptive power of creative personality would shatter all patterns. Continuously crashing to the ground, towers of Babel would destroy all order. Transmission of ideas, customs, skills, and values from one generation to another would cease.

Without conservative forces to counteract the disruptive effects of creativity, man could not exist as both an individual and a member of society. Part of the paradox of the creature a little lower than God comes to focus here. Every man must at one and the same time be an unduplicated individual and a near duplicate of his fellows.

Society not only functions to socialize and transmit ideas through time, it also nurtures a host of conservative forces. Just as the individual is the source of the new, so society is the guardian of the old and established. Every group, institution, and social unit must have its own pattern of the normal and accepted. Were this not the case, society and its institutions could not be preserved for even one generation.

A basic human dilemma, and not mere prejudice, was involved in official resistance to novel proposals of the Savior and his followers. Adherents of the established system were forced to make a fundamental choice. They could not listen to Jesus *and* hold their old loyalties unaltered. They were forced either to make sweeping adjustments in their institutions or to reject new teachings. This factor elevated religious change to a life-and-death issue. Stephen was stoned because he said Jesus of Nazareth would "change the customs which Moses delivered to us." (Acts 6:14)

44

Bloodshed is the ultimate defense against change.

Next to physical violence, laughter is perhaps society's most potent weapon with which to guard the old and accepted against threats from the new and proposed.

Harald Høffding suggests that "The mere possibility of employing laughter as a weapon shows that it involves the idea of power." Without making a formal analysis of that power, Israel's prophets and poets have recognized its central role in human affairs. Few descriptions of ridicule match the vividness of these lines from the Psalter:

> . . . I am a worm, and no man;
>> scorned by men, and despised by the people.
> All who see me mock at me,
>> they make mouths at me, they wag their heads.
>> —Psalm 22:6-7

Centuries later, Charles Darwin was struck by the fact that when a man laughs in the face of another, he shows his teeth. Such an act, in the opinion of the naturalist, represents a holdover from days when men expressed anger by snarling and baring their canine teeth.

Darwin's estimate must not be taken too seriously, for it was influenced by his passion to find evidence for his theory of organic evolution. Still, it is suggestive. Without being concerned with biological considerations, Henri Bergson pointed out that many types of laughter serve to intimidate by humiliating.

Tamar, daughter-in-law of Judah, was a central figure in the sex-centered drama reported in Genesis, chapter 38. After enticing the tribal elder into adultery, she took his signet, cord, and staff as security for payment of a kid. Judah kept his word and sent the kid—but his agent could not find the woman. Much as he would have liked to recover his personal gear, Judah preferred to drop the matter without more inquiry. " 'Let her keep the things as her own,' he insisted, 'lest we be laughed at. . . .' " (Genesis 38:23)

Even when trivial issues rather than moral standards are involved, likelihood of laughter is a major factor influencing decisions. Staff members of a denominational agency in Nashville, Tennessee, gathered some months ago to hear a distinguished visiting speaker. After ceremonies were under way, the chairman announced that someone had forgotten to turn off his car lights, but had locked the doors. He read the tag number of the car in question; someone snickered, and the whole group broke into a laugh.

Still, no one moved to cut off the lights. Puzzled, the chairman described the car so that it could be identified. With an explosive burst, one member of the group waved her arms and started to the parking lot: "It's mine! It's mine! Go ahead and laugh!"

When dramatized before two hundred persons, so simple a matter as having forgotten to turn off car lights becomes a source of real embarrassment. Because we want to be considered normal and not eccentric, all of us fear laughter. We often choose to be despised or hated, in preference to being ridiculed. In some respects, a person who evokes laughter is branded as impotent—incapable of threatening those who mock him. So to be the object of continuous public mockery is to occupy one of the lowest of social hells.

Only prophets and philosophers are likely to be interested in formal analysis of that laughter which suppresses individual tendency to deviate. But in every epoch, all groups and institutions have employed it as a weapon. So long as men can be held in check by jeers, it is not necessary to muster troops.

46

Sanballat, an officer under the Persian government, was solidly opposed to Nehemiah's proposal that Jerusalem's walls be rebuilt. At first, however, the official did not prod Samaria's garrison into armed attack. With his allies, the angry defender of things as they were launched a campaign of ridicule:

"And he said in the presence of his brethren and of the army of Samaria, 'What are these feeble Jews doing? Will they restore things? Will they sacrifice? Will they finish up in a day? Will they revive the stone out of the heaps of rubbish, and burned ones at that?'" (Nehemiah 4:2-3; cf. 2:19.)

Just such reactions have challenged every champion of change. In modern Western culture, the weapon employed is likely to take the form of a cartoon or joke. Viewed from so short a distance as one century, many of the jeers at Abraham Lincoln by his contemporaries seem less humorous than cruel. Issue after issue of the *Review of Reviews* preserves fossil political cartoons directed against the "liberalism" of Woodrow Wilson. In similar vein, some crafty opponents of alcohol control fought proposed legal changes by telling jokes.

According to one of these stories, a noted temperance lecturer concluded his hard-hitting talk by giving a demonstration. Lifting two glasses from the table, he dropped a worm in each. Then he took great pains to point out that the worm in the water was swimming, while the worm in the alcohol had died. Climaxing his argument, he called: "What does that mean, my friends?" From the rear of the hall came a mellow voice: "It means that if you drink enough liquor, you'll never be troubled with worms."

Part of the pervasive power of such a verbal weapon lies in the fact that many persons tend to enjoy a joke for its own sake. Therefore some who advocate alcohol control may tell such a story—or laugh at it—without recognizing that they undermine their own position.

Changes that would lead to reform, which is a turning back of the social clock, are likely to be fought zealously. Hence the reformer is as frequent a target for jibes as is the trail blazer.

About 700 B.C., Assyrians invaded and conquered Israel. Judah made an uneasy peace by surrender and payment of tribute. In both lands there was a strong Egyptian party whose members urged coalition with the southern kingdom against Assyria. After a generation of chaos and unrest, King Hezekiah proposed a reform in the religious system. Instead of suggesting radical new patterns of worship, he launched a crusade to return to earlier and better ways by celebrating the Passover.

Did his royal edict win immediate popular acceptance? By no means! ". . . couriers went from city to city through the country of Ephraim and Manasseh, and as far as Zebulun; but they laughed them to scorn, and mocked them." (2 Chronicles 30:10)

Whether employed by authorities trying to suppress a popular movement or by masses who resist proposed reforms, laughter in support of the *status quo* is a variable. Its nature is not constant, but varies from group to group and occasion to occasion. That is the case even when social control involves no more than "doing things the way they've always been done."

Deviation from custom evokes chiding laughter from persons assembled for any familiar activity. An incident not noticed at the ball park can throw a congregation into stitches. Norms of the two occasions are not the same; therefore, laughter does not erupt in like fashion. A practice taken for granted at a baseball game may be decidedly eccentric in a house of worship. So a listener who leaned forward in his pew and cheered the choir would be humiliated, even crushed, by laughter of his fellow worshipers. Local nature of such controls is indicated by the fact that shouting and jumping about were habitual in frontier camp meetings, so drew no restraining snickers.

If you wish to experience for yourself the tremendous power of social control through laughter, try an experiment. In plain view of forty men and women on an airliner, walk into a rest room just vacated by a member of the opposite sex. Chances are that you can return to your seat without so much as one raised eyebrow.

Then try the same thing before a group of men and women assembled for a committee meeting or dinner. Operating with greater restraining power than a shouted threat, gales of laughter will say to the man who accidentally opens the door to the ladies' room: "Stop! You are violating accepted standards!"

Jesus recognized the significance of laughter as a restraining force, and urged every would-be disciple to count the cost before rushing to adopt new ways. "Otherwise, when he has laid a foundation, and is not able to finish, all who see it begin to mock him, saying, 'This man began to build, and was not able to finish.'" (Luke 14:29)

It is one thing deliberately to adopt a course that will bring laughter upon one's head. It is quite another thing to blunder into such a situation—and beat a hasty retreat when thrown into the fearful isolation of standing up to face ridicule of a group.

Because God's revelations frequently stir men toward change, the teacher or leader or prophet who proclaims late word from on high can expect to be a target for laughers. By no means fully reconciled to the ostracism that greets such a spokesman, Jeremiah lamented:

49

> I have become a laughingstock all the day;
> every one mocks me. . . .
> For the word of the LORD has become for me
> a reproach and derision all day long.
>
> —Jeremiah 20:7f

Recognition of social forces involved in such laughter is one step toward mastering them. For the advocate of change or reform who is self-consciously yielded to God, gains from him power to resist pressure toward conformity. This is the path to victory such as proclaimed in Psalm 119:51:

> Godless men utterly deride me,
> but I do not turn from thy law.

Derided by colleagues because he challenged ideas of the day, Job found strength to resist the hammering of their ha-ha chorus.

> "Bear with me, and I will speak,
> and after I have spoken, mock on," he told them.
>
> —Job 21:3

Not in spite of the fact that it is radical, but precisely because it challenges the customary, a deep truth of religion may get nearly universal mockery. As we shall see in our survey of institutional laughter directed at the Savior, threat of change is likely to evoke jeers whose intensity mounts with seriousness of the challenge. It is for this reason that the concept of divine judgment has been the butt of laughter during many centuries.

Modern sophisticates sneer at the notion of "pie in the sky, bye and bye." But their laughter is not new. Peter felt it necessary to warn early Christians about this matter.

"First of all you must understand this, that scoffers will come in the last days with scoffing, following their own passions and saying, 'Where is the promise of his coming? For ever since the fathers fell asleep, all things have continued as they were from the beginning of creation.'" (2 Peter 3:3-4)

In every culture and under all circumstances, change has so fearful a face that many members of a group use laughter to defend things as they are. This process plays a vital part in preservation of society, for unchecked tendencies to deviate could wreck the social structure. Yet this necessary brake upon the wheels of change must not be regarded with too great awe. That pioneer who is conscious of being led by God, thereby gains courage to challenge the *status quo* even when he is all but overwhelmed by laughter in support of things as they are.

5

THE MOCKERY OF JESUS

No aspect of laughter in the Bible is more significant, or has had less attention, than the mockery of Jesus by his own.

It is not difficult to discover the basis of that reaction. Just as society in general employs laughter as a weapon to defend the *status quo,* so every institution—including the religious—relies upon mockery to resist change.

Representing as he did the supreme instance of radical challenge to men and institutions, Jesus constituted a supreme threat. So laughter directed at him had to pass far beyond giggles that restrain those who depart from custom at the level of the trivial.

Greek philosophers recognized the basic dilemma by saying that "Truth can be like the light to sore eyes." Since that is so, supreme truth embodied in and communicated by the Son of God was necessarily a supreme source of challenge—and not merely a petty annoyance.

According to Luke's chronology, which has much to support it at this point, Jesus' public ministry was launched in a gale of derisive laughter. Accustomed to regarding the gospel story as dead serious, we fail to hear that laughter unless we stand in the shoes of first-century listeners.

Step into the synagogue in Nazareth with mingled curiosity and skepticism. You are here because everybody in town has been talking about the return of Jesus. It will be good entertainment to hear what this local yokel will presume to say. . . .

Jesus reads from the Book of the prophet Isaiah. It is not accidental, but of crucial importance, that he selects an inflammatory passage. From the first word, it is apparent that this is no casual reading. Everything in the voice, facial expression, and gestures of Jesus serves to underscore the revolutionary character of his definition of mission:

"The Spirit of the Lord is upon me,
because he has anointed me to preach good news to the poor.
He has sent me to proclaim release to the captives
and recovering of sight to the blind,
to set at liberty those who are oppressed,
to proclaim the acceptable year of the Lord."

—Luke 4:18-19

Fine words, they are. But look who dares to wave them before us as a battle flag! Such a threat to overturn everything that we know would be a signal to draw our weapons and attack—if the speaker wore armor and had fighting men at his back. Since that is not the case, this mighty mouther of fine words, this potent champion of wind, can be overthrown without exchange of blows. We will send him packing, with no weapon except laughter!

"Where did this man get this wisdom and these mighty works? Is not this the carpenter's son? Is not his mother called Mary? And are not his brothers James and Joseph and Simon and Judas? And are not all his sisters with us? Where then did this man get all this?" (Matthew 13: 54-56)

Held at arm's length by their jeers, Jesus made little impact upon men of his home town. That is the only recorded instance prior to Passion Week in which masses of common folk so doubted and mocked that the Savior could do no mighty works.

There are indications, however, that on some occasions before the climactic closing days of his ministry, Jesus was taunted and derided by religious officials. Light is thrown upon these incidents by behavior of chief priests and scribes who made a holiday of the crucifixion. There they went through the act of asking for what they regarded as an impossible "sign," or proof of the carpenter's claims.

No genuine request for light, the demand was an inverted kind of jest—a broad practical joke calculated to evoke many a wink and snicker. With mock seriousness that every man recognized to be ridicule, foes of Jesus talked loudly among themselves: " 'He saved others; he cannot save himself. Let the Christ, the King of Israel, come down now from the cross, that we may see and believe.' " (Mark 15:31-32)

Just such a denouement was foreshadowed earlier. Scribes and Pharisees who requested signs received an abrupt refusal. Its tone suggests that Jesus considered the

54

request less than serious. Those who made it were not really eager for evidence that would make them believe. Instead, they taunted the man who would change the Sabbath and other customs by asking him to do things they considered impossible. He scored such pretended piety as indicative of "an evil and adulterous generation" (Matthew 12:39), promised no sign except the enigmatic one of Jonah.

Scoffing and mock requests for signs were at the level of preliminary skirmishes. Powerful attacks through ridicule and physical torment were reserved for closing days of the battle between Jesus and champions of the established institution. That such an outcome was inevitable, he indicated before starting on the final journey. " 'Everything that is written of the Son of man by the prophets will be accomplished,' " he warned his disciples. " 'For he will be delivered to the Gentiles, and will be mocked and shamefully treated and spit upon. . . .' " (Luke 18:31-32)

This calculated campaign of laughter—integral to events that brought salvation to men—assumed ominous tones when Jesus was seized. It was not enough to plot the death of this disturber of the peace; he must be humiliated and turned into a laughingstock so men would not take him seriously. Tension in the house of Caiaphas was therefore relieved by a comic interlude. "Now the men who were holding Jesus mocked him and beat him; they also blindfolded him and asked him, 'Prophesy! Who is it that struck you?' " (Luke 22:63-64)

Viewed through eyes of fervent faith, that incident evokes shudders rather than laughter. Precisely because that is the case, it indicates the gravity of first-century mockery. In cruel and brutal fashion, Jesus' foes deliberately tried to persuade men that he was a clown. It was not enough that he should die; a dead hero is often more dangerous than a living one. He had to become an object of ridicule, so men would laugh at his memory. To that end, the final climactic mockery of Jesus centered in a series of three incidents involving three representative groups.

Roman soldiers, symbolizing the power of the political institution, had their field day first. Because the times were rough and these men lived by the sword, gentle twitting would have evoked no laughter. There had to be the sight of blood and the sound of fists upon flesh.

> Then the soldiers of the governor took Jesus into the praetorium, and they gathered the whole battalion before him. And they stripped him and put a scarlet robe upon him, and plaiting a crown of thorns they put it on his head, and put a reed in his right hand. And kneeling before him they mocked him, saying, "Hail, King of the Jews!" And they spat upon him, and took the reed and struck him on the head.—Matthew 27:27-30.

At Golgotha there came the punch line of the farce by which the eternal empire of Rome tossed dust into the face of a petty Galilean who dared challenge Caesar's power. Having crucified this petty rebel, soldiers had the biggest laugh of all. For as his life ebbed away, they put over his head the legend: " 'This is Jesus the King of the Jews.' " (Matthew 27:37)

Rome had had her fill. There was no longer anything funny about this pretender.

Then came the common folk of Israel, sons of Abraham, seed of God's chosen people. At first, they had been impressed with the claims and message of this strange young descendant of David. Now, it was obvious that they had been deluded. So they must strike back, retaliate, save face.

What better way to do it than to show their superiority by treating the Galilean as a futile, impotent object of laughter?

> And those who passed by derided him, wagging their heads and saying, "You who would destroy the temple and build it in three days, save yourself! If you are the Son of God, come down from the cross."—Matthew 27:39-40.

Third and last in the parade of those who stabbed with fierce jokes were the representatives of the religious institution. Here, in a sense, was the focus of the entire issue. This self-styled spokeman for God had made leaders of the temple look ridiculous. Very well, he must die to the sound of triumphant laughter.

> So also the chief priests, with the scribes and elders, mocked him, saying, "He saved others; he cannot save himself. He is the King of Israel; let him come down now from the cross, and we will believe in him. He trusts in God; let God deliver him now, if he desires him; for he said, 'I am the Son of God.' "—Matthew 27:41-43.

Those who took leading parts in this first-century holiday must have gone home, still smiling at the great practical joke they had played, proud of the way they had turned the tables upon a revolutionary. Twenty centuries later, you and I need to pause and take a long second look before joining the chorus of those who mock a crusader or reformer. Savage beneath its gay exterior, much loud laughter is protest against accepting the transforming word of a messenger from God.

6

A FALSE GOAL WHEN PURSUED
FOR ITS OWN SAKE

Seeking firsthand experience that would help him select meaningful goals, the Preacher examined both wisdom and folly. He quickly concluded such a pursuit to be mere chasing after wind. So he took a new path:

> I said to myself, "Come now, I will make a test of pleasure; enjoy yourself." But behold, this also was vanity. I said of laughter, "It is mad," and of pleasure, "What use is it?" I searched with my mind how to cheer my body with wine—my mind still guiding me with wisdom—and how to

lay hold on folly, till I might see what was good
for the sons of men to do under heaven during
the few days of their life.

· · · · · · · · · · · · · · · · · ·

And whatever my eyes desired I did not keep
from them; I kept my heart from no pleasure,
for my heart found pleasure in all my toil, and
this was my reward for all my toil. Then I considered all that my hands had done and the toil
I had spent in doing it, and behold, all was vanity
and a striving after wind, and there was nothing
to be gained under the sun.—Ecclesiastes 2:1-3,
10-11.

Few sections of Scripture are less congenial to the modern
mind than is Ecclesiastes. It is small wonder that this
powerful and disturbing little book is often pushed aside
as obscure and profitless. Really to examine the philosophy
it expresses is to challenge some basic assumptions on
which twentieth-century Western civilization rests.

One contemporary point of view, seldom challenged,
assumes that laughter is a good thing—a worthy object of
pursuit in its own right.

Humor is among the most eagerly sought commodities
offered on the American market. We not only buy humor
today; as a culture, we buy it at premium prices. Any person who can guarantee a steady flow of laughter is relieved
of all merchandising problems. His wares are so greatly
in demand that prospective purchasers will seek him out
and eagerly bid against one another for a portion of his
output.

As the most highly paid person in his society, the professional entertainer is something new under the sun. Every
age and culture has had its laugh-makers. But few have
elevated them to the status of cultural hero.

59

Medieval crusaders, for example, had comparatively little time and money for those who spent their days concocting laughs. Life objectives of the era largely came to focus in recapture of the Holy Land from the infidel. Warriors who fought under the cross laughed, of course. They valued the services of the jester. But in contrast to modern Westerners, they did not elevate laugh-makers to top positions in society. Prestige and earning power of court fools were quite different from that of Hollywood clowns and television buffoons.

There are strong reasons to doubt that any other culture has seen anything like the present proliferation of commercialized laughter.

Not until this generation were there so many media of mass communication to serve as channels of transmission, it is true. But that is not the whole story. We laugh often and loudly at made-up humor, not only because it is readily available but also because we are all but frantic in our eagerness to get it.

From *Post* cartoons to after-dinner speeches, from humorous signs for office desks to television comedies and animated cartoons, those things that make us laugh are appreciated partly because . . . they make us laugh.

Such laughter is likely to be hollow, lacking in many qualities that attach to the joy of great souls who found delight in God. As a nation, contemporary America strikes one as being lavishly entertained—but not especially joyful. No number of weeks in Miami Beach or Las Vegas can quite confer those intangibles that permitted Israel to sing:

This is the day which the LORD has made;
let us rejoice and be glad in it.

—Psalm 118:24

Differences are more easily recognized than specified. But that laughter which comes as a fruit of deliberate seeking has a different ring from laughter that emerges spontaneously. The distinction almost serves as an index to some cultural goals and values.

Our willingness to pay any price for a carefully tailored gag suggests that we'd rather laugh at life's inscrutible mysteries than be overwhelmed in pondering them. Much commercial humor is empty and contrived, valued chiefly because it provides a false face that camouflages life's tragedy. Concentrating upon the grinning mask of a fool, we spare ourselves the painful task of viewing grim aspects of our human predicament.

Uncertainty, finitude, and bewilderment vanish under the intoxicating effects of laughter. Punch waves his magic wand. A mellow glow so dominates that for an instant—at least one jolly instant—there is no consciousness of surrounding darkness, blurring of the divine image, and the tragedy of less than the best.

If this view of laughter pursued as a prize seems strangely out of step with the times, that is partly because our culture finds the biblical outlook somewhat alien. We pride ourselves upon the place Scripture holds in our society but, as a people, we do not devote significant time and energy to meditating upon its central messages.

Because those messages have to do with God and men, and because men have no activity more characteristic than laughing, the Bible has much to say about pursuit of a good time. Many passages point to the danger of seeking laughter as a goal to be gained apart from the delight of coming to know God.

In ancient times, as in modern, much striving for the mellow mood was linked with alcohol or some other drug. That was far from being universally the case, however.

Any brief treatment of so complex a subject as the biblical view of wine and strong drink is necessarily over-simplified. Among the scriptural writers, there are a variety of emphases. Almost without exception, those who contributed pungent sayings and noble ideals to "wisdom literature" took a "moderate" view. Yet they were scathing in their condemnation of drunkenness.

Prophets generally took a more severe view of wine than did writers of proverbs and poems. Priests habitually used fermented juice of the grape in their rites and ceremonies. It was not considered inappropriate, but wholly right and proper, to employ light wines upon the most sacred and solemn occasions. Among no class of Israel's leaders was there ever a concerted crusade comparable to the prohibition movement in the United States.

Most who pondered the ways of God and revealed their insights to their fellows, espoused moderation. They had nothing but condemnation for drunkards, yet they could not be called ascetics.

Quite a different situation seems to have prevailed among the masses of common folk. As a nation, Israel never lost her sense of mission as a chosen people. Yet during generation after generation, hosts of her citizens drank in order to experience the effects of alcohol. That such was the case is clearly indicated by warnings that otherwise would have no reason to exist:

Wine is a mocker, strong drink a brawler.

—Proverbs 20:1

Summarizing an epoch of national bliss in 1 Kings 4:20, the historian reports that "Judah and Israel were as many as the sand by the sea; they ate and drank and were happy." At least a part of that drinking was from the cup that cheers—after a fashion.

Cultural success, defined as "eating and drinking," had so many adherents that the Preacher was forced to reckon with it as one of the goals a man might deliberately select. It was a commonplace saying, frequently repeated with little or no thought, that

> Bread is made for laughter,
>   and wine gladdens life,
>   and money answers everything.
>
> —Ecclesiastes 10:19

That formula was quoted only in order that it might be refuted. Divine approval or condemnation aside, actual physical weal and woe were linked with sobriety and indulgence. To all who seek laughter in a bottle, the Preacher thunders:

> Woe to you, O land, when your king is a child,
>   and your princes feast in the morning!
> Happy are you, O land, when your king is the son of
>   free men,
>   and your princes feast at the proper time,
>   for strength, and not for drunkenness!
>
> —Ecclesiastes 10:16-17

Such warnings, never silenced, would not have been uttered had there not been persistent pursuit of wine-warmed moods. Though they had no precise formulas to indicate the strength of a brew and were without psychological theories to account for alcoholism, Israel's thinkers knew quite well how intoxicants affect their users. It was taken for granted that strong drink distorts one's outlook, bending impressions and ideas in the direction of fantasies that afford temporary escape. That many of Abraham's descendants were prone to become tipsy suggests that frenzied striving for some variety of "peace of mind" is not so modern as it sometimes appears.

Scripture includes more than 300 references to wine and strong drink, plus half as many allusions to vines and vineyards. It was a matter of paramount importance that the Promised Land to which God led his own was rich and productive, "a land of grain and wine, a land of bread and vineyards" (2 Kings 18:32).

It is useless to attempt to explain away such references by suggesting that the people of the Book used alcohol only as a food. To them it was a major food item, of course. But that was not its only role. Some valued it as a significant, albeit false, path toward gaiety. No prophetic attack upon winebibbing gives a more vivid indication of popular attitudes than does the little-known fable of the trees seeking a king.

Abimelech having slaughtered his own kinsmen in order to seize the throne, the masses applauded. Only his youngest brother, Jotham, survived to resist. In a futile attempt to persuade the men of Schechem that their choice was an evil one, he told his own version of a fable that must have been in general circulation.

> "The trees once went forth to anoint a king over them; and they said to the olive tree, 'Reign over us.' But the olive tree said to them, 'Shall I leave my fatness, by which gods and men are honored, and go to sway over the trees?' And the trees said to the fig tree, 'Come you, and reign over us.' But the fig tree said to them, 'Shall I leave my sweetness and my good fruit, and go to sway over the trees?' And the trees said to the vine, 'Come you, and reign over us.' But the vine said to them, 'Shall I leave my wine which cheers

gods and men, and go to sway over the trees?'
Then all the trees said to the bramble, 'Come
you, and reign over us.' And the bramble said to
the trees, 'If in good faith you are anointing me
king over you, then come and take refuge in my
shade; but if not, let fire come out of the bramble
and devour the cedars of Lebanon.' "—Judges
9:8-15

Note that elevation of the bramble came only after the
royal office had been refused by the olive, fig, and vine.
It is the language used by the latter in rejecting the offer
that is here significant. Haughtily the vine declines:

" 'Shall I leave my wine which cheers gods and men, and
go to sway over the trees?' "

Popular recognition of so high a status for the vine indicates that multitudes did not share the severe views of
prophets and reformers. To the latter, laughter linked with
fruit of the vine actually represented delight in degradation.

For a little while, the tipsy herdsman played the role of
hero in a world whose problems were no longer too big for
him. Transformed by wine, he seemed to himself suddenly
to be victor over his limitations. So long as his alcoholic
world did not crash upon his head he could—as he saw it
—strut about in such invincible fashion that he could make
fun of every challenger.

Hence it was not strange that on some occasions, men
deliberately got drunk so the transformed self might engage
in some daring act. Sober, restraining forces were taken
seriously. Full of wine, they took on a different aspect and
might be defied to the tune of strident laughter.

Naomi, wise in the ways of the flesh, knew that Boaz
could not fail to find Ruth good to look upon. But she also
knew quite well that there was a great gulf between a
wealthy Hebrew and a Moabite widow. It would take a

special situation to induce Boaz to ignore convention for the sake of her comely daughter-in-law.

So Naomi gave specific instructions to the girl. Having washed and anointed herself, Ruth put on her best clothes and went down to watch the men winnowing barley. As instructed, she stayed in the dark shadows until their work was finished, watching for the right moment to approach her quarry.

> And when Boaz had eaten and drunk, and his heart was merry, he went to lie down at the end of the heap of grain. Then she came softly, and uncovered his feet, and lay down. At midnight the man was startled, and turned over, and behold, a woman lay at his feet!—Ruth 3:7-8

It would be straining the sense of that vivid story to conclude that Boaz was drunk. Yet it would also be a distortion to ignore the fashion in which wine affected his mood and therefore his response to the overtures of the foreign woman.

Biblical writers, realists in depicting conduct and keenly aware of alcohol's power to work transformations, show that even kings took this path to hilarity. So long as he was sober, Ahasuerus had too much respect for his queen to use her as the butt of a joke.

In the third year of his reign, however, he threw a royal celebration. His officers and staff chiefs were entertained for 180 days. Then he gave a seven-day banquet for the general public, with all the people of the capital invited into the courtyard of the palace.

> There were white cotton curtains and blue hangings caught up with cords of fine linen and purple to silver rings and marble pillars, and also couches of gold and silver on a mosaic pavement of porphyry, marble, mother-of-pearl and precious

> stones. Drinks were served in golden goblets,
> goblets of different kinds, and the royal wine was
> lavished according to the bounty of the king.
> And drinking was according to the law, no one
> was compelled; for the king had given orders to
> all the officials of his palace to do as every man
> desired.—Esther 1:6-8

Freedom to drink as much or as little as might be desired
may reflect a concession to views of reformers. For the king
himself seems to have had no scruples—and a burning
thirst. On the final day of the orgy, when Ahasuerus was
merrily alcoholic, he thought it would be great fun to give
his guests a laugh by exhibiting his queen. So he sent his
seven chamberlains to bring Vashti before the company
"with her royal crown, in order to show the peoples and
the princes her beauty; for she was fair to behold." (Esther
1:11)

Vashti refused to come. Her tipsy husband, thrown into
a rage, set in motion the events that led to the dramatic
climax described in the Book of Esther.

Kings were not alone in making rash decisions after
becoming merry with wine. At the other end of the power
scale, rebels and revolutionaries used alcohol to break down
barriers of fear and respect for rulers. In preparation for a
revolt against the authority of King Abimelech, Gaal the
son of Ebed gathered a band of malcontents and won their
confidence.

> And they went out into the field, and gathered
> the grapes from their vineyards and trod them,
> and held festival, and went into the house of their
> god, and ate and drank and reviled Abimelech.
> And Gaal the son of Ebed said, "Who is
> Abimelech, and who are we of Schechem, that
> we should serve him?"—Judges 9:27-28

In somewhat different fashion from scewing up the courage of a revolutionary band, Absolom used wine to transform personality. Instead of drinking it himself, however, he depended upon the certainty that his foe would consume too much. Seeking revenge for Amnon's sexual assault on his sister Tamar, Absolom arranged a banquet. Apparently he was unwilling and his men were afraid to strike with everyone cold sober.

> Then Absalom commanded his servants, "Mark when Amnon's heart is merry with wine, and when I say to you, 'Strike Amnon,' then kill him. Fear not; have I not commanded you? Be courageous and be valiant." So the servants of Absalom did to Amnon as Absalom had commanded.—2 Samuel 13:28-29

Not all such accounts include a report of alcoholic laughter. But whether men drink in order to make merry, or laugh because they are less than sober, false hilarity is linked with ancient drinking bouts as well as modern ones.

There actually are parallels between impact of alcohol and those divine agencies that also transform personality. That is part of the pernicious effect of pursuing wine-soaked laughter. Some who come to enjoy it accept it as a substitute for that personality-changing intoxication which is a fruit of encounter with God.

It was not incidental, but vital, that even before his birth the son of Zechariah should be recognized as unconventional. His deviation from accepted patterns was a result of divine visitation, however. Dull ones might easily confuse his enthusiasm with effects of drink. So the angel who announced his birth clearly stipulated the source of his less than sober ways:

68

" . . . he will be great before the Lord,
and he shall drink no wine nor strong drink,
and he will be filled with the Holy Spirit,
even from his mother's womb."—Luke 1 : 15

Root meanings of the word *enthusiasm* ("inspiration or possession by a god") are significant here. Adoption of such a term by the Greeks served to underscore some parallels between effects of deep religious fervor and the fruit of the vine. Both alcohol and the Holy Spirit have radical, unpredictable, transforming effects. They take men to quite different terminals, of course. But "possession by God" and drunkenness are alike in that both do lift men out of themselves for a time.

Man's very yearning to escape himself as he is, constitutes one mark of the divine. In wishing change, the restless are altogether right. Some err, not in the urge to become other than what they are, but in seeking those changes symbolized by laughter over wine.

Mirth of that sort, unlike the laughter of joy at the goodness of God, does nothing to induce growth of the mind and spirit. Instead, it serves as an anesthetic. Those who revel in drunken chuckles succeed only in degrading themselves and offending God.

Through Hosea, God rebukes Israel for having played the role of faithless wife. She has gone off after other gods, and divine retribution will include stripping her of her merriment and the vineyards that help produce it.

"Now will I uncover her lewdness
    in the sight of her lovers,
    and no one shall rescue her out of my hand.
And I will put an end to all her mirth,
    her feasts, her new moons, her sabbaths,
    and all her appointed feasts.

69

And I will lay waste her vines and her fig trees,
   of which she said,
   'These are my hire,
      which my lovers have given me.'
I will make them a forest,
   and the beasts of the field shall devour them."
                              —Hosea 2:10-12

Whether imbibed culturally or individually, alcohol works its transforming effects only temporarily. When sobriety returns, things may look entirely different. Witness the case of the churlish and ill-behaved Nabal, rich shepherd of Maon.

At the time of shearing, he curtly rejected David's courteous plea for food. Abigail, his wife, learned of the matter and acted without his knowledge. While he drank himself into a stupor, she loaded food upon animals and sent a caravan as a peace offering to David and his armed forces. Though the young commander forgave Nabal's insult, he admitted that had Abigail not acted as she did, the whole tribal group would have been slain.

> And Abigail came to Nabal; and, lo, he was holding a feast in his house, like the feast of a king. And Nabal's heart was merry within him, for he was very drunk; so she told him nothing at all until the morning light. And in the morning, when the wine had gone out of Nabal, his wife told him these things, and his heart died within him, and he became as a stone.—1 Samuel 25:36-37

Cold sober, the world is far from identical with that which seems to surround one who has found laughter in a bottle. If the "good humor" of an alcoholic jag is a token of empty and futile change, an accompaniment of striving for false goals, what shall we say of other ways in which laughter is sought as an end in itself?

Clearly, the same general conclusions hold. Drink is by no means unique as a producer of empty laughter. It is simply the most accessible and most common instrument with which to achieve a fanciful state of victory and hilarity.

Many persons actively seek that special kind of laughter that stems from winning success in the material realm. Peter's scathing indictment of false prophets and heretical teachers links them with just such a point of view. They promise their followers a jolly good time here and now; "Do not be concerned about the future, it will take care of itself," they say.

> They count it pleasure to revel in the daytime. They are blots and blemishes, reveling in this dissipation, carousing with you. . . . For, uttering loud boasts of folly, they entice with licentious passions of the flesh men who have barely escaped from those who live in error. They promise them freedom, but they themselves are slaves of corruption; for whatever overcomes a man, to that he is enslaved.—2 Peter 2:13, 18-19

One does not have to be immoderate in his use of wine to be completely absorbed in tangible goals. Absorption with a good time here and now can so dominate the mind that concern for future reward vanishes.

It is in this sense that twenty-century yearning for laughter of security constitutes a symptom of social sickness. Though he might express it differently, the life goal of many a modern is like that of the rich fool derided by Jesus. When one accepts such a goal as final, it is an exclamation of victory to say: "Soul, you have ample goods laid up for

71

many years; take your ease, eat, drink, be merry." (Luke 12:19)

From night club revues to after-dinner speeches, from pornographic magazines to clever sayings of children, from jaunty sketches to dull old stories told by preachers, anything that is good for a laugh is "valuable" in contemporary Western culture. So frenzied is our pursuit of laughter by which we can escape from ourselves that much of it is sordid, brutal, or bestial.

Whether we admit it to ourselves or not, most of us know in our hearts that a hearty guffaw can drown out the still, small voice. We are so very eager for laughs that we will erase the image of the Creator and descend to subhuman levels, if necessary, in order to make merry.

At the St. Louis Zoo on a day in early spring, the keeper at the monkey house fell into conversation with visitors. They inquired about the dangerous animals, and he explained that he himself was actually afraid of the baboons.

"And I suppose the animals aren't the only problems. Those boys who are teasing the chimpanzees must give you trouble."

"Oh, not much. They're just pretending to throw popcorn, with empty hands to see the chimps hunt it. It's the adults who give us the real trouble. They like to play practical jokes on the animals, and the bigger the crowd, the louder they laugh. Sometimes we go a whole week without an incident. Then there's a whole rash of 'em. Grown men and women throw flash bulbs and lighted cigarettes into the cages so the crowd can get a laugh."

Recognition that so brutal a pattern of behavior is a perennial problem to zoo keepers is sufficient to revive the familiar fable of monkeys who came to view the haunts of men.

With contemporary Christians as with ancient Hebrews, even those who are pricked into spiritual unrest may be prone to settle for the anesthetic of easy laughter. So it is necessary that the seeker for God turn the power of laughter upon itself and through irony challenge those who value laughter too highly to ask what it is they are really pursuing.

It is in this vein that the Preacher jerks us up short by offering in mock seriousness this summary of life's meaning: "I commend enjoyment, for man has no good thing under the sun but to eat, and drink, and enjoy himself, for this will go with him in his toil through the days of life which God gives him under the sun." (Ecclesiastes 8:15)

In biblical times as well as modern, many a man accepted enjoyment at face value, and devoted his life to pursuit of a good and comfortable time. Whether he emits audible chuckles or not, that person who feels he has "arrived" may be in so merry a mood that he ceases to seek God. Such spiritual failure has much in common with that which stems from seeking gladness by way of drink.

That is why the witness of Scripture includes so many unqualified condemnations of those processes that foster the pursuit of laughter as a goal in itself. Laughter has dignity and validity only when it emerges as a by-product of worthy striving. Sought for its own sake as a sort of spiritual sedative, it becomes degrading.

7

ARMOR
TO PROTECT THE EGO

Life is unbelievably complex. You and I are so limited, so small when seen against the backdrop of the universe about us, that we continually become involved in problems too big for us. Life's demands require that we often ignore them and pretend we are not puzzled by them—or admit our limitations and engage in creative outreach.

Laughter is intellectual armor with which men may protect themselves when challenged by the new, unknown, and never before experienced. One who laughs may succeed in pushing a mystery or marvel aside, denying that it exists. Such a reaction eliminates the necessity for mental and spiritual change. It therefore fosters complacency, pride, and self-assurance.

One of the most intriguing of all instances of biblical laughter serves as a case history from which to examine this matter. In his old age, Abraham came into personal meeting with God. He accepted with holy fear the divine promise of a covenant whose terms made him the father of many nations.

But the mood of the patriarch changed when God indicated specific factors involved in the fulfillment of the covenant. Such wholly illogical things would happen to Sarai, God told Abraham, that her name must be changed to Sarah in order to symbolize the transformation. As a result of divine blessings, she would become a mother of nations by bearing a son in her old age.

No man could listen to such a message from on high without vigorous response. Abraham might have reacted in a mood of joy, praising God for his incredible goodness. But that would have required him to modify all his firmly fixed notions about the age at which men and women become parents. So instead of bursting into ecstatic praise, Abraham rejected the proposal and protected himself from having to modify his own ideas. As the climactic incident is described in Genesis 17:17-18,

> Then Abraham fell on his face and laughed, and said to himself, "Shall a child be born to a man who is a hundred years old? Shall Sarah, who is ninety years old, bear a child?" And Abraham said to God, "Oh that Ishmael might live in thy sight!"

In earlier chapters, we have noted that no one laughs at a joke until he understands it—gets the point. Some American jokes about doughnuts are incomprehensible in England, because they focus upon holes—and English doughnuts do not have holes. One who laughs, thereby

75

symbolizes that he is master of the situation. He understands the matter under analysis, and is in a relationship of superiority.

Abraham was so bowled over by God's ridiculous proposal that he couldn't keep his feet! He rocked with merriment, "fell on his face and laughed." By doing so, he gave vivid evidence that he considered himself to have a joke on God. He witnessed to his own superior understanding of the situation—and thereby protected himself from the necessity of asking whether his set of "answers" about parenthood were so fixed and final as he assumed them to be.

Thomas Hobbes went so far as to trace all laughter to "sudden glory arising from some sudden conception of some eminency in ourselves, by comparison with the infirmity of others, or with our own formerly." So viewed, smiles and chuckles are tangible symbols of victory. Just as they erupt when one solves a riddle or suddenly achieves a touchdown, they accompany any situation of abrupt conquest.

Such an interpretation of laughter is much too narrow. Obviously it does not apply to all instances in the Bible or out of it. But the fault of the theory may lie in Hobbes's making too broad an application of it, rather than in its validity for a limited portion of laughter's spectrum.

Goliath, the Philistine of Gath, recognized that it was no light matter to step before an army and challenge foes to singlehanded combat. For each man who assumed the role of champion of his forces, the issues involved were life and death. It was a sober and tragic occasion when two men caught sight of one another for the first time as they prepared to take the outcome of battle upon their individual shoulders.

But when Goliath got his first good look at David, he could not remain sober. He reacted by triumphant mockery. His disdain for the ruddy and comely youth was such that he considered the duel won before it started. So he engaged in uproarious taunting:

> And the Philistine said to David, "Am I a dog, that you come to me with sticks?" And the Philistine cursed David by his gods. The Philistine said to David, "Come to me, and I will give your flesh to the birds of the air and to the beasts of the field."—1 Samuel 17:43-44

Can't you hear the big man guffaw as he hurls these rib-tickling insults? For him, the occasion is one of hilarity—because he rejoices in the discovery that his opponent is weak and puny. Goliath is safe; he faces no real threat. Therefore he can deride his foe, and that publicly.

Spiritual and intellectual consequences of such triumphant laughter are tremendous. For it is an easy refuge and a stout shield against many kinds of challenge. Calling for zeal to resist the influence of ungodly men in the church, the brief letter of Jude traces their views to rebellion in proud ignorance: "these men revile whatever they do not understand." (Jude, verse 10)

Any man who is stirred and challenged is likely to respond in serious fashion rather than by ridicule. It is only when a challenge is not recognized as potent, when it is assessed and rejected as a threat to one's status, that laughter is likely. We do not laugh when we see the unusual as unusual; we laugh when we regard ourselves as having mastered the new, the mysterious, the never before encountered.

It is not strange that some intellectuals of Athens mocked when Paul talked to them about resurrection of the dead.

(Acts 17:32) That was precisely the reaction of mourners when Jesus himself challenged the certainty of their understanding of life and death. Pushing his way into the circle of those weeping and bewailing Jairus' daughter, the Master challenged all their established certainties by saying the girl was not dead, but sleeping. "And they laughed at him, knowing that she was dead." (Luke 8:53)

Even for a moment to consider the possibility that they lacked full understanding of death was too much. These folk had wailed at many a funeral. They were experts. They had neatly catalogued systems of knowledge so firmly fixed that rearrangement was incredible. So they laughed to make it clear that they knew more about death than this teacher from Nazareth, and to underscore the fact that they did not intend to re-examine their views. At one stroke, their laughter served to protect them in their position and to indicate their superiority over Jesus.

Piety tends to look with disgust and pity at these knowing ones—experts because they are professionals in mourning. In their limitedness, they dared to consider their understanding absolute. They put themselves on record as having the final answer. They laughed at the very concept of "miracle."

We so easily shake our heads in pity at their blindness— and in the same breath that we cluck our sympathy for them, we catalog our own absolutes. Of course, many a list is beautifully camouflaged: "It would be inconsistent with the character of a loving Father to do thus and so. . . . Because we know God is absolutely just, we can be sure he would not behave thus and so. . . ."

Let us be done with the whole empty mockery. Let us recognize that we cannot know or define God or his works —in history or outside it. "Impossible" is a human, but not a divine category. To laugh because we are comfortably certain of what God cannot do is to retreat within a fortress of pride so that we will not have to take a fresh look at our own ideas.

This is no light matter. God was affronted by laughter at his promise made to Abraham.

> The LORD said to Abraham, "Why did Sarah laugh, and say, 'Shall I indeed bear a child, now that I am old?'" Is anything too hard for the LORD? At the appointed time I will return to you, in the spring, and Sarah shall have a son." But Sarah denied, saying, "I did not laugh"; for she was afraid. He said, "No, but you did laugh."—Genesis 18:13-15

From the perspective of centuries, it is easy to pity the blindness of Abraham and Sarah, the spiritual emptiness of those who mourned in Jairus' house. But when we look at the problem of using laughter as armor with which to protect smugness in our own lives, it is easier to see the dilemma than to escape from it.

Bernard of Clairvaux was a bitter opponent of all heresies. His preaching is credited with having launched the second crusade in 1147. His sermons and theological works earned him the title, Doctor of the Church. In the light of his preoccupation with such weighty topics, it may seem strange that he should have pondered the significance of laughter that serves to shut out challenges. But in a powerful analysis as pertinent to our century as his, Bernard makes "Foolish Mirth" the third step of pride.

He who is in this way seldom or never will be heard sighing or seen weeping. You would think, to watch him, that he either had no conscience or else had no sins to be conscious of. Facetiousness appears in his gestures, merriment in his face, vanity in his stride. He likes to make jokes; he is easily and quickly moved to laughter. Everything contemptible, and therefore unpleasant, which he knows in himself is erased from memory. He gathers together the good things, if he finds any in himself, or else creates them in the mind's eye . . . he compresses his lips, he grinds his teeth; he laughs without wanting to, he guffaws involuntarily. And when he blocks his mouth with his fists, you can hear him chortle through his nose.[1]

Whether an habitual response in challenging situations or an outburst at the notion of God's accomplishing the impossible, defensive laughter is likely to be empty. It lacks some indefinable but recognizable qualities of the laughter of pure merriment. More than one Oriental observer of modern Western life has commented upon the prevalence of surface laughter among some peoples. A Chinese analyst put it like this: "Americans are not happy; they laugh too much."

Even to raise such an issue is to invite angry refutation. For in all ages and not simply the contemporary West, there have been many who habitually jeered in order to avoid having to think. Such a person, challenged to examine his scoffing, is likely to respond by snarling.

He will not go to the wise.—Proverbs 15:12
A scoffer does not like to be reproved;
He who corrects a scoffer gets himself abuse,
and he who reproves a wicked man incurs injury.

—Proverbs 9:7

To sit in the seat of the scornful is to occupy a mental/spiritual mood oriented 180° away from "delight in the law of the LORD" (Psalm 1:1). One outlook is comfortable and closed. The other is challenging and open. Con-

---

[1]From Bernard of Clairvaux, *The Steps of Humility;* George B. Burch, Trans. Cambridge: Harvard University Press, 1940, p. 201-203. Used by permission.

sequently it is not strange, but wholly logical, that

A scoffer seeks wisdom in vain,
   but knowledge is easy for a man of understanding.
                                             —Proverbs 14:6

That person sheltered by a breastwork of jeers, whose armor of laughter deflects divine messages that would prick him into radical change, is all but invulnerable. There is no way to get through to him. Tennyson expressed the idea tersely in *Idylls of the King*. "Mockery," he said, "is the fume of little hearts." Such hearts are little precisely because they have mocked—and rejected opportunity for growth.

It follows that from time to time you and I will do well to take a mental step backward and examine an instance of personal laughter. Seriously to ask, "Why did I laugh?" or "What is there here that impels me to laugh?" is to open doors that lead to creative change. Something of this idea is hinted in the formula of James:

Draw near to God and he will draw near to
you. Cleanse your hands, you sinners, and purify
your hearts, you men of double mind. Be
wretched and mourn and weep. Let your laughter
be turned to mourning and your joy to dejection.
—James 4:8-9

H. L. Mencken once ventured to suggest, "Human life is basically a comedy." Such a view is completely alien to the biblical outlook, according to which creatures made in the image of God have nobler tasks than spending their lives in pursuit of laughter. Among God's own, it is not right even to talk of low things, warns Paul. "Let there be no filthiness, or silly talk, nor levity, which are not fitting." (Ephesians 5:4)

81

Such pursuits, innocent as they often seem, may constitute avenues of retreat from God. For there is no outward sign that matches laughter as an index to the closed mind. On levels far below that of sublime issues of life and death, where Scripture's messages focus, history gives numerous instances of mockery that in the end showed nothing but limitedness of the mockers.

When Walter Scott began his boyish attempts to write by jotting down a few lines of poetry, his father did his best to discourage him. "These unprofitable flights of your fancy will lead you nowhere," he warned.

High school teachers considered Honoré de Balzac to be stupid, so made fun of him to his face. "This fat little fellow goes around in a state of intellectual coma," one of them said.

When W. C. Durant predicted that some day 500,000 autos would be made yearly in the U. S., financial expert George W. Perkins, partner of J. P. Morgan, scoffed: "If he has any sense, he'll keep those notions to himself when he tries to borrow money!"

Whether in the realm of transportation, literature, or man's relationship with God, transformation hinges upon active belief. Lacking willingness to examine altogether incredible new alternatives, there is no basis for creative outreach. Let us be slow to slam a door in the face of God by laughing at messages which require us to change in order to accept them.

8

AN INDEX TO GOALS, VALUES, AND BELIEFS

In some circles it is no longer fashionable to talk about visions. Any reference to conversation with angels is likely to produce a reaction ranging from pity to disgust—almost any emotion except reverent wonder. Imagination is permitted to run riot as a technical civilization dreams about space travel, but in many circles it is bad form to discuss divine revelation.

Perhaps this situation is neither so new nor so strange as it appears at first glance.

Long ago, the patriarch Lot took up residence in the city of Sodom. By many modern standards it was not so much a city as a crossroads village. But it was famous—or infamous—as the ancient equivalent of a wide-open town. People of Sodom were frank in their dedication to gross and sensual pleasure. If there were no commercial honky-tonks, it was because none were needed; almost every roof covered a house of iniquity.

Miracle of miracles, Lot held himself aloof and refused to be tarred with filth of his neighbors. Undoubtedly, he spent much time in searching his soul as to what he should do. At last he received a warning so vivid and startling that he could only regard it as sent by God.

Bursting into action, he hurried to tell his loved ones of the warning he had received from the Lord's own representatives. " 'Up,' " he urged, " 'get out of this place; for the LORD is about to destroy the city.' " (Genesis 19:14)

It was useless. Even in an epoch given a glow by distance, so that it appears to have been more reverent and attentive to God than our own era, Lot had difficulty getting a hearing. There is no doubt about his own fervor. But instead of striking terror into the hearts of all whom he warned, he provoked some of them to laughter: " . . . he seemed to his sons-in-law to be jesting." Though his words fell on their ears, they did not receive and accept his message.

A major trend in our time is increasing attention to communication. Rise of such new media as radio and TV has contributed to this development.

Several decades of intensive study have yielded some rather conclusive findings. Among them is a new concept of the role played by persons on the receiving end. In order for communication to take place, there must be readers or hearers. Far from being passive, the receiver plays a part that is just as vital as that of the writer or speaker.

This means that effective communication may be blocked at either of two points.

Everyone is familiar with the first: awkward or inept use of words by the person on the sending end. Given a speaker who loses in the struggle to find effective words in which to convey his ideas, listeners squirm as the clock grows more and more listless in shifting its hands.

This problem is quite distinct from that of producing fresh and challenging ideas. No matter how vigorous one may be as a thinker, he faces the tremendous task of using words in such fashion that his ideas can enter the minds of others.

A second roadblock is linked with the person on the receiving end. Given a listener or reader who lacks skill in handling words and other symbols, there can be no effective exchange of ideas. If it falls on deaf ears, a brilliant and provocative message will fail to get an appropriate reaction. No speaker can pour ideas through ears of his listeners in the fashion that water is poured through a funnel. "Failure" of a sermon or church school lesson or lecture may stem as frequently from actions and attitudes of a listener as from shortcomings of the leader.

It was a bungled attempt to "soften up" an audience by laughter that started a contemporary minister upon his quest for new understanding of the listener's role. Webb B. Garrison says that the impetus for his volume on *The Preacher and His Audience* came from a single incident.

Speaking to personnel of an Alabama air base, the Methodist minister had a routine week until Saturday morning. That day, "character guidance lectures" were scheduled in the base auditorium—and attendance was mandatory. "You can imagine how enthusiastic the men were about coming on Saturday morning to listen to a visiting preacher," he recalls.

Since the auditorium would not hold the entire group, two identical lecture sessions were scheduled, one at 8:00

85

A.M. and the other at 9:00. According to Dr. Garrison, the first hour was routine. Men who made up his audience were polite—they had to be. They did not get up and walk out, physically. But early in the hour many of them filed out, mentally.

Everyone involved recognized the situation, so, at the beginning of the second session, one of the chaplains decided he would create a better speech situation. He set about doing so by the technique many ministers and public speakers use: telling half a dozen jokes and anecdotes having no connection with the theme or occasion.

Everything went well for the first two or three stories. Most men smiled, and some laughed aloud. Then the chaplain launched into a vivid account of the adventures and misadventures of one whom he called "a darky preacher." His Negro dialect was excellent, and the race-linked joke was funny from some perspectives. But he had not reached the punch line before static electricity had the air live with tension: nearly half the men in the audience were Negro.

In three or four sentences, the speaker tried to relate his message to the problem of race relations in the United States. Then he gave the same lecture as before. This time, however, response was quite different. No one nodded, and many listened intently. Several came up at the end of the hour to express their appreciation.

"It was the same message, but a different audience," he declares. "A single piece of explosive humor transformed an indifferent audience into an eager one—with many hostile, and others curious. This incident sent me home to spend many months trying to analyze the strangely-neglected question of the listener's role in communication."

As suggested in earlier chapters, this matter is particularly significant as an index to response in laughable situations. When listeners are not skilled in handling a speaker's symbols, there is no capacity to "see the point" of a joke or jeer that is deliberately used in an attempt to provoke laughter.

Today it would lead to bewilderment rather than laughter for a political candidate to call his opponent a Locofoco. But in 1844, Whigs used that mocking label for Democrats in order to get a laugh. That was because in 1844, everyone knew that a locofoco match flares brightly but may burn the hand of the man who holds it. Lacking a handle by which to grasp the term, "locofoco" is not even meaningful—to say nothing of being laughable.

Conversely, the typical reader of 1844, not having been exposed to elementary chemistry and being unacquainted with formulas for water and sulphuric acid, would frown in bewilderment at a jingle that "sends" today's high school students:

> We had a little Willy;
> Now Willy is no more.
> For what he thought was H_2O
> Was H_2SO_4.

What is true for recognition of allusions based on chemical formulas and use of matches applies to experience in general. Laughter is a major index to goals, values, and beliefs. By our laughter, we signal that we understand and are masters of the situation—though an observer might recognize that understanding on a high rather than a low level would lead to a reaction quite different from laughter. The notion of a child's confusing sulphuric acid and water is funny only when regarded as a joke rather than a real situation.

It is no small consolation to recognize that even so earnest and godly a man as Lot found it difficult to transmit his message. He was burning with a divine warning—but when he put it into words so it could be shared with others, he met ridicule.

Lot's sons-in-law laughed because they accepted his warning only on a superficial level of meaning. Thereby they indicated that they lacked beliefs and experiences necessary for grasping the full import of his message. Though they were physically mature, these men were spiritual babes. Not yet having mastered addition and subtraction, they were suddenly exposed to algebra.

To them, Sodom seemed a normal city that in no way deserved the wrath of God. So though words were exchanged with their father-in-law, there was no communication. Winking at one another, the young men tapped their heads significantly and laughed aloud at the notion of fleeing from the city. They considered themselves urbane, not knowing their laughter actually showed them to be "wretched, pitiable, poor, blind, and naked." (Revelation 3:17)

Scientific study of communication is a modern development. But the importance of listening from the proper point of view was recognized long ago. Scripture includes many references to this matter. Over and over, men are described as having ears but failing to hear, having eyes but being incapable of seeing truth.

In his immortal *Confessions,* Augustine recognizes that he cannot prove to his readers the truth of what he says. "But," insisted the fifth-century spiritual giant, "they whose ears charity doth open unto me, they believe me."

A listener's point of view is like a filter used by a camera enthusiast; though it does not change the outside situation, it has great influence upon the inner picture. Deep-seated beliefs, values, and even emotions of the passing moment serve as filters in communication. "To the pure all things are pure, but to the corrupt and unbelieving nothing is pure; their very minds and consciences are corrupted." (Titus 1:15)

In literal fashion, wants and attitudes sometimes bend sounds toward the familiar or the desirable. Tennyson has a stingy old gentleman listen to the "clop, clop, cloppety-clop" of a horse's hooves and hear them saying: "Property, . . . property, . . . property."

Many of the laughable "blunders" made by children grow out of their limited experience. Exposed to an unfamiliar word, they may distort it in their minds so that it is heard as a familiar one. A church school teacher discovered this phenomenon when she asked small children to draw sketches of famous persons in the Bible. One boy drew a uniformed airman in the cockpit of a plane. Questioned, he explained that it represented "Pontius the Pilot."

Because their knowledge of God and his ways made them spiritual children, Lot's message conveyed no vital meaning to his sons-in-law. Instead, it seemed to point to incompetence and incoherence on his part. Surely the old gentleman couldn't be serious; he must either be losing his mind or trying to pull a joke!

Though the biblical record includes no details, Lot's sons-in-law may have been affected by their nearness to him. It is hard enough for ordinary folk to grasp the import of a God-sent message that is delivered by some noted stranger. It is all but impossible for most of us to recognize divine elements in a message delivered by someone very familiar.

Florence Nightingale was absolutely convinced that her call to a career in nursing came from God. To her, the message was as clear and unmistakable as was the warning which prompted Lot to speak. But the high-born English girl received no better treatment than did Lot.

Mrs. Nightingale, far from taking her daughter seriously, was inclined to ridicule the pretensions of "poor Florence." She discussed the girl's dreams with her aristocratic friends, half-apologized for what she felt would prove a passing fancy. It never seemed to occur to her that a child reared in her own home could have something vital to say to society. She would have scoffed at the notion of gaining her own place in history through the reflected glory of her queer daughter, so abnormally concerned with the sick.

We must not be too vigorous in condemning this woman. From the viewpoint of a later era, she seems to have been incredibly silly and blind. But the backward look is very different from the forward. Once a new idea wins general acceptance, it takes neither originality nor courage to look back at it and say, "How obvious!"

Regardless of its nature, almost any unconventional idea is likely to be ridiculed so long as it retains the shine of novelty. Tendency to laugh is probably more or less proportional to the degree of originality in a startling message. Especially when the message comes from an unlikely source —such as a member of one's own circle of relatives and friends—it is easier to scoff than to ponder.

God respects no man-made conventions. He can and does speak through all kinds of persons. Some of his most stirring messages are delivered through men whom their neighbors would never consider likely candidates for the prophet's mantle. Poor, humble men have often served as channels for transmission of divine truth. Equally strange, so have rich and powerful men.

In the year that King Uzziah died, the Lord touched the heart of a young aristocrat. Isaiah was filled with wonder and fear. Supernaturally cleansed and thereby given capacity to see and hear in fresh fashion, he emerged with a vital message. But he was warned to expect misunderstanding.

Any literal translation of subtleties expressed in verse is likely to raise problems. That is especially the case here. Mockery and derision are not mentioned as such; yet they are implied in God's unqualified condemnation:

> And he said, "Go and say to this people:
> 'Hear and hear, but do not understand;
> see and see, but do not perceive.' "
>
> —Isaiah 6:9

Instead of being awakened by Isaiah's challenges, his hearers will become more indifferent than ever. They will respond to his loud, clear call in the way men react to the continuous clamor of a bell: after a time, they cease even to notice it. So part of the prophet's role is to dramatize public rejection of his message. Humorous overtones spring from daring metaphors that make hearts "fat" and ears "heavy," underscoring recognition that Isaiah's hearers have no intention of making the effort required to understand:

> "Make the heart of this people fat,
>   and their ears heavy,
>   and shut their eyes;
> lest they see with their eyes,
>   and hear with their ears,
> and understand with their hearts,
>   and turn and be healed."
>
> —Isaiah 6:10

Years earlier, God demonstrated his power by calling a messenger from the most unlikely of places: the inner sanctum of the religious institution. Young Samuel, trained under Eli, was impelled to denounce the powerful old ecclesiastic. He knew what God wanted him to say, but dreaded the saying. "And Samuel was afraid to tell the vision to Eli." (1 Samuel 3:15) Yet the power of the message was sufficient to transform the messenger. God used a boy to bring sweeping reforms in Israel's religion when men listened to Samuel, understood, and acted on his challenge.

In a different but equally effective way, divine meanings flowed through the life of a rough herdsman from Tekoa. Amos differed from Samuel, and Samuel had few qualities in common with Isaiah. God used each of them. His messengers are not all of a type, easily and surely recognizable. Rather, he works through a great diversity of persons. Any eager girl, zealous young scholar, or unlearned old father-in-law—however strange the possibility—may actually transmit late news from God when men hear him with understanding ears.

Neither formal learning nor lack of it, poverty or wealth, youth or age, high station or low, distance or proximity, nationality or race, health or illness can constitute an insuperable barrier to God. John Bunyan, tinker, spoke for God as have few Englishmen except John Wesley, Oxford scholar. Paul of Tarsus, a frail Roman citizen perpetually troubled by a thorn in the flesh, was a messenger whose only peer was the impetuous big fisherman whom Jesus called to be a fisher of men.

God's messengers are of so many sorts that we dare not judge any message by the man who bears it.

Whenever groups or individuals pay more attention to who a person is than to what he says, storm clouds are brewing. Lot's sons-in-law refused to take his message seriously.

"Listen to the old fool!" one of them may have snickered. "Here he is, chattering about this God of his. God never has bothered Sodom. Why should he interfere now? Let's go tell the fellows, and let them enjoy a laugh, too!"

Just such a response has greeted many of the world's great prophets, outside the realm of religious values as well as within it. Even in so work-a-day a field as transportation, many a novel idea has been greeted with bursts of laughter.

In 1836 the learned Dr. Dionysius Lardner poked fun at the notion of crossing the Atlantic in a steamship. No vessel could carry enough coal, he said—and proved the point by a mathematical demonstration. Copies of his twenty-five-page treatise were carried to America on the *Sirius,* first steam-powered vessel to cross the ocean.

To mention the Wright brothers is to recall the waves of ridicule that greeted their idea of building a flying machine. Experts joined the general public in laughing at such foolish notions. Hence the first magazine article on their work was published, not in a technical journal, but in *Gleanings in Bee Culture.* Other editors were so positive the plan was absurd that they wouldn't even consider publishing material about it.

It is clear that much laughter stems from ignorance or from total inability to appreciate a novel idea. Ridicule of a message, whether it is linked with a sense of divine commission or not, may condemn the hearer rather than the bearer.

Some men are continually ready to laugh at the unfamiliar. They keep their laugh mechanism cocked, ready to go off at the slightest touch. Any fresh idea will trigger an explosive burst of ridicule.

> As the crackling of thorns under a pot,
> so is the laughter of the fools.
> —Ecclesiastes 7:6

Such laughter bursts into prominence very quickly and produces a momentary flash of heat. But it is very poor fuel with which to fire the stewing pans of a culture. It burns out so quickly that ideas are seldom brought to the boiling point.

Few men in Israel's early history provoked so much laughter as did Elijah. He was a religious enthusiast of the first order—a man so intoxicated by his zeal for God that he neglected the ordinary conventions of society. Even the children made fun of him. Their laughter at the queer fanatic, the eccentric "baldhead," doubtless echoed the verdict of their elders. For in any era, those who do not wish to hear a message that would remake society are likely to defend themselves by mocking the Elijahs of their day.

Even the Bible has no life-transforming message for those who are unwilling or incapable of reading with eyes that see. There is no beauty in any piece of music for the man who does not or cannot listen with appreciation. Greatest paintings are but daubs of color to those who cannot or will not view them with sympathy and interest.

To laugh at a canvas by Whistler or a symphony by Beethoven is to indict, not the creator, but the judge of the masterpiece. Every challenging idea should be examined on its own merits rather than ridiculed without consideration. Laughter that is too quick and glib often serves to condemn the hearer rather than the bearer of a message, however bizarre, that is offered as a revelation from on high.

Radical transformation of one's scale of values, brought about by encounter with God through one of his messengers, may turn laughter inside out, as it were. " 'Truly, truly, I say to you, you will weep and lament, but the world will rejoice; you will be sorrowful, but your sorrow will be turned into joy.' " (John 16:20)

Prefaced by the formula for emphasis, this significant analysis of human reactions underscores dichotomy between those of the world and those who are conscious of having been chosen by God. Exposed to an emotion-charged situation, members of the two groups react in opposite fashion. This is an aspect of the way in which Jesus' message, instead of judging men enables men to pass judgment on themselves by their reactions.

This almost hints that those events which evoke joyous mirth on the part of men whose lives are centered upon material goals, should automatically evoke lamentation from those who fervently seek the kingdom and have a degree of maturity in their understanding of its values.

All communication, including laughter, involves two-way processes. Listeners play as dynamic and vital a role as do speakers. God follows no set pattern in selecting persons to bear his messages to men; he can use any dedicated life whatever. So a fresh idea or novel point of view should be considered on its merits rather than on the prestige of the person who offers it. Shallow-minded persons who jeer at authentic word from God, condemn themselves and bring down fire from heaven upon their own heads.

9

A CATALYTIC AGENT
IN SOCIAL CHANGE

The claims adjuster for a big transit company sent for a woman who had lost a thumb in a trolley accident.

"Madam," he demanded firmly, "don't you see that your claim of $5,000 for a single digit is ridiculous?"

"Not at all," she explained. "This was no ordinary digit. It was the thumb that I kept my husband under."

Circulating in half a dozen versions, that story brought laughs from audiences in the United States who heard it early in the twentieth century. Vocal response to the yarn tended to vary in direct proportion to the number of husbands in a given audience.

96

Used in a skit addressed to a group made up entirely of wives, the story would be unlikely to evoke more than a few polite smiles—and might be greeted with icy silence. Offered to an audience of medieval craftsmen or Bantu tribesmen, it would be rejected as meaningless. For only in contemporary Western society with its pattern of dominance by women in many areas, does that story of a thumb have special dynamic.

It represents a padded weapon, which males brandish to challenge the role of women. Instead of publishing a pamphlet or seeking to have a bill introduced into Congress, men tell stories making fun of the accepted cultural pattern. Used in that fashion, humor is a catalytic agent that fosters social change. From gentle satire to ridicule whose words hit like bludgeons, verbal weapons have been employed in every age by persons and groups seeking to stir complacent ones into revising their ideas.

To call the role of those who have employed laughter as a weapon of attack would be to enumerate the great and near-great in most fields of thought. Thorstein Veblen used biting satire to challenge complacency of the clergy, whom he derided in *The Theory of the Leisure Class*. Using the misadventures of Don Quioxote as a vehicle through which to pour his criticism of an era, Cervantes made men laugh in order to make them think.

Multitudes who never dream of reading a book of political science are stirred by Kipling's story of "The Village that Voted the Earth Was Flat." Aesop's Fables would be regarded as inflammatory if their conclusions were advanced through more sedate literary vehicles. And Jesus of Nazareth was one of the world's great masters of humor as a pin with which to prod the minds of men. So vast and important is the stream of humor in the gospel record that it must be treated separately, in Chapter 10.

Challenging the use of humor in the pulpit, a contemporary analyst has suggested that "You cannot heehaw people into the kingdom of God." Few would debate that issue. But full-bodied mockery has had a place in the prophetic witness of some whose words have found permanence in Scripture.

In the classic contest between Elijah and the prophets of Baal, the stage was set by preparation of two bulls ready for sacrifice. After the 450 pagan priests had called upon Baal from morning until noon without result, Elijah drew the sharp knife of ridicule from his belt:

> at noon Elijah mocked them, saying, "Cry aloud,
> for he is a god; either he is musing, or he has gone
> aside, or he is on a journey, or perhaps he is
> asleep and must be awakened."—1 Kings 18:27

That the biblical writer was conscious of the role played by laughter is indicated by his report that Elijah's foes "limped about the altar which they had made." (1 Kings 18:26)

Whether he had Elijah's jibes in mind it is impossible to say. But when Paul matched wits with sophisticates of Athens, he, too, resorted to use of humor. It was this speech element, in fact, that he used to catch attention and challenge thinking of those who heard his famous sermon in the Areopagus. Beginning with sarcasm, he quickly moved on to interpret his own faith in positive fashion:

> "Men of Athens, I perceive that in every way
> you are very religious. For as I passed along, and
> observed the objects of your worship, I found
> also an altar with this inscription, 'To an un-
> known god.' What therefore you worship as
> unknown, this I proclaim to you."—Acts 17:
> 22-23

Much in the messages of Israel's prophets would probably have overtones of satire and ridicule, if we had sufficient familiarity with background conditions to recognize humorous elements. In the case of Amos, even a twentieth-century dweller in an industrial civilization can see that the herdsman used wit as a weapon. He must have spoken primarily to groups of oppressed persons, else his life would hardly have been safe after such a blast as:

"Hear this word, you cows of Bashan,
    who are in the mountain of Samaria,
who oppress the poor, who crush the needy,
    who say to their husbands, 'Bring, that we may drink!'
The Lord GOD has sworn by his holiness
    that, behold, the days are coming upon you,
when they shall take you away with hooks,
    even the last of you with fishhooks."

—Amos 4:1-2

That characterization of the *grandes dames* of Israel's upper crust probably represents a high watermark in biblical invective.

Most reformers in secular history as well as in sacred have used ridicule as a weapon. That is particularly obvious in the case of central figures in the Reformation, the Renaissance, and the rise of Humanism. Nearly all economic and political revolutions involve generous use of laughter directed at the old order. Both the French and the American revolutions produced some of the world's great satirical literature, and it flourished in the tense climate that preceded the U. S. Civil War.

Pascal went so far as to suggest that prophets and reformers make deliberate rather than incidental use of laughter. It would vastly improve society, he said, if saints would habitually make fun of human folly for disciplinary purposes!

Whenever such a program is adopted, it has the effect of revealing customs and values in a new light. Laughter functions as an ultraviolet lamp, under whose rays familiar things may take on radically different appearance. Jesus marveled at the centurion who so far surpassed the descendants of Abraham, Isaac, and Jacob in capacity for life-giving faith. But the Roman officer had the advantage of hearing the gospel call as absolutely fresh; he saw it in a new light.

Always, it is difficult or impossible to discover the transforming power of a system of belief or value when a watered-down version of it is dominant and familiar. It is necessary to lose sight of the conventional view in order to gain a vantage point from which to see radical new truth. Laughter has great power to provide such perspective, because it shatters the taken-for-granted so that pieces can be reassembled in fresh fashion.

That is the basis of such parodies as the materialist's version of Psalm 23. Written by Edward K. Ziegler, a minister, of Roanoke, Virginia, it was widely circulated a few years ago.

Science is my Shepherd,
  I shall not want;
He maketh me to lie down on foam-rubber mattresses;
He leadeth me beside six-lane highways.
He rejuvenateth my thyroid glands;
He leadeth me in the paths of psychoanalysis for
  peace of mind's sake.
Yea, though I walk through the valley of the shadow
  of the iron curtain, I will fear no communist; for
  thou art with me; thy radar screen and thy
  hydrogen bomb, they comfort me.
Thou preparest a banquet before me in the presence
  of the world's billion hungry people.

Thou anointest my head with home permanents.

My beer glass foameth over.

Surely prosperity and pleasure shall follow me all the
  days of my life; and I will dwell in Shangri-la
  forever.[1]

Commenting on these lines in *The Christian Century,*
Halford Luccock recognized that many readers would consider them blasphemous. But he suggested that such razor-
edged wit frequently serves to cut intellectual and spiritual
knots that would not yield to a dull weapon such as
straightforward, prosaic argument or sermonizing.

In less obvious but equally keen fashion, the writer of
Genesis told humorous stories to challenge complacency of
material-minded ones. B. Davie Napier distinguishes four
such anecdotes in *From Faith to Faith.* Once his keen ear
has heard and identified laughter in these familiar accounts, we can listen with him and hear for ourselves.

Genesis, Chapter 23 is an intriguing case history of
oriental bargaining. Seeking a burial place for Sarah,
Abraham enters into negotiations with the Hittites. With
excessive politeness, they insist upon giving him a piece of
ground. Abraham eventually confesses that the plot he
wants is the cave of Machpelah, but it is not until ceremonial bargaining has been completed that the purchase
price of four hundred silver shekels is named.

According to Napier, this ancient story clearly suggests
by its literary form that it circulated orally long before it
was committed to writing. Humor of the excessively polite
negotiations must have been a source of pleasure to both
the teller of the story and those who listened. But it was
humor with a sting—making fun of ceremonial politeness
of business deals.

---

[1]Used by permission of the author.

Having completed his purchase, Abraham promptly set out to make another. He sent his oldest and most trusted servant to negotiate for a wife for Isaac. Soon the emissary made contact with Rebekah; as a reward for her courtesy in giving him water, he gave her a gold ring and two gold bracelets.

Back home, the girl babbled her story to the whole family. Laban, her brother, did not hesitate. "When he saw the ring, and the bracelets on his sister's arms . . . he went to the man; and . . . said, 'Come in, O blessed of the LORD; why do you stand outside?' " (Genesis 24:30-31)

Laban's exuberant cordiality, spurred by ten and one-half shekels' weight of gold jewelry, was no more laughable than a similar reaction on the part of Jacob, years later. He arrived in Laban's area and paused beside a big well whose mouth was covered by a stone so heavy that it was customarily moved by several shepherds. Natives of the region pointed out Rachel to him, and told him that the sheep she tended belonged to her father, Laban. Jacob moved into action in dramatic style, without waiting for others to lend a hand with the big stone:

> Now when Jacob saw Rachel the daughter of Laban his mother's brother, and the sheep of Laban his mother's brother, Jacob went up and rolled the stone from the well's mouth, and watered the flock of Laban his mother's brother. Then Jacob kissed Rachel, and wept aloud.—Genesis 29:10-11

Whether Jacob's burst of strength came as a result of seeing Rachel, or was stimulated by the sight of the flock she tended, the ancient storyteller does not specify.

For his own part, Laban was quick to greet Jacob when he learned his identity as heir of the wealthy Abraham.

" 'Surely you are my bone and my flesh!' " he exclaimed (Genesis 29:14). After Jacob's visit had lasted a month, Laban protested against continuing to accept his guest's labor, gratis. They should have a formal understanding, he said. So they entered into a contract by which Jacob would work seven years for Laban and be paid by receiving Rachel as his bride.

For ancients who told and retold this cycle of stories, the mockery of materialism probably reached its climax in Jacob's marriage. For crafty Laban exchanged his daughters on the wedding night and palmed off weak-eyed Leah upon the son of Abraham. Both Laban and Jacob were out to take advantage of one another, and they seesawed back and forth in a battle of wits that must have made Israel's shepherds laugh until they held their sides with pain.

Whether it be greed attacked in the Abraham-Jacob saga, excessive concern with science mocked in the technological version of the Shepherd Psalm, Amos condemning social decay in Israel or Jonathan Swift conducting eighteenth-century Englishmen along the path of Gulliver's travels, the nonconformist who employs laughter may be misunderstood. If he is not, he is likely to be subjected to bitter counterattack. Provided that the sting of his humor is sufficiently powerful, he may even become a martyr because of it.

Defensive laughter, serving to defend the *status quo,* has been analyzed in Chapter 4. Yet we must recognize here also that the prophet, the reformer, or the innovator is likely to be the subject of derision even if he himself doesn't deliberately employ humor.

Do not reprove a scoffer, or he will hate you;
reprove a wise man, and he will love you.

—Proverbs 9:8

103

Anger, if not actual hatred, is likely to be the defense mechanism of any who are complacent and cynical. Jesus' biting story of the dishonest steward evoked jeers from some who heard it. Attacked at the point of their love for money, the Pharisees "scoffed at him." (Luke 16:14)

Many who participated in strange events of the day of Pentecost, without having a background of belief in the new gospel of Jesus Christ, were bewildered and stirred to seek explanations. "But others mocking, said, 'They are filled with new wine.'" (Acts 2:13)

Paul recognized that some who listened to his impassioned addresses, made fun of him on the score that "'his bodily presence is weak, and his speech of no account.'" (2 Corinthians 10:10)

It is not strange, but entirely natural, that the counter-attack to nearly every proposal for innovation should include laughter. For this is an almost involuntary response to a really prophetic message.

Oriented forward rather than backward, humor is among the most potent of all social forces—an adjunct of the revolutionary principle itself. In his introductory comments to the monumental collection, *A Treasury of Satire,* Edgar Johnson goes so far as to declare that "Satire is a powerful civilizing agent: if we ever become civilized it will probably be satire almost as much as poetry that will have accomplished it."

10

JESUS' USE OF HUMOR

In his analysis of *The Secret of Laughter*, Anthony M. Ludovici spoke for many readers of Scripture when he insisted that "there is not a joke in the whole of the New Testament."

Obviously there is nothing in the account of Jesus' life and message that is funny for the sake of being funny. Yet when one listens to the Master's words with ears attuned, it is impossible to escape recognizing that his message flows from a life that is rounded and full—not lopsided or distorted.

Already we have seen that laughter is so pervasive and varied that it is a basic human activity. That being true, it seems that careful scrutiny would reveal not one but several streams of laughter in the message and mission of the Savior.

Fulton J. Sheen, in *Lift Up Your Heart,* goes so far as to suggest that the gospel message itself can be described as "the doctrine of the Divine Sense of Humor." As he interprets that idea, the saving sense of humor means: "Nothing in the world is to be taken seriously—nothing except the salvation of a soul. The world, and the things that are in it will one day be folded up like an Arab's tent; you are not to live exclusively for this life."

Regardless of whether or not you are willing to adopt such a point of view, attentive reading of the gospel record reveals that Jesus certainly did have a well-developed sense of humor. In fact, he employed humor in such a variety of ways and upon so large a scale that it can be regarded as a major element in his recorded teachings.

To recognize and interpret laugh-provoking factors in Jesus' message, it is necessary both to adopt first-century viewpoints and deliberately look for elements that enter into humor. To facilitate the latter process, it will be helpful quickly to summarize some foundations from which laughter often springs.

Since the time of Aristotle, great minds have pondered not only the functions of laughter in society but also the bases on which humor rests. At least four principles are generally recognized.

(1) *Disparagement* is a basis for much humor. There is an almost universal tendency to laugh when an unaffiliated person is made to look stupid or ridiculous. Even accidents and brutality produce guffaws. This is perhaps linked with the fact that laughter enhances the position of the laugher by lowering the status of its object.

106

(2) *Superiority* on the part of the laugher is therefore linked with disparagement of the laughee. When one chuckles over the physical buffets suffered by a clown, he is saying in effect: "That fellow is very stupid to walk into the side of an elephant in such fashion. I would not do it, for I am more intelligent than he."

(3) *Release from suppression* seems to be a third major source of laughter. Whenever authority is made to look ridiculous, a potentially humorous situation exists. No other theory accounts for the way in which persons of varied cultural background laugh at stories which violate standards. A joke that taps a repressed desire is always more explosive than one whose humor rests on an impulse considered noble or honorable. Thus, the moonshine whisky industry is a more fruitful source of Yankee jokes than is the patriotic impulse.

(4) *Incongruity* serves as a base for much humor. This factor is obviously related to feelings of superiority. The person who "gets the point" unconsciously congratulates himself upon his own quick wit.

Importance of this factor is indicated by humor in nonverbal media. Music alone—without title or program— can evoke laughter. Sudden contrast, or incongruity in sound patterns, seems to be the most distinct source of such humor.

It is unlikely that even the simplest instance of laughter will stem from a single factor. All four of these basic ingredients may be involved in a one-sentence witticism or a brief anecdote. Hence the attempt to explain a particular laugh as due to some one clearly defined cause is likely to be futile.

Disparagement, superiority, suppression, and incongruity are not constant elements. Rather, they vary from individual to individual, and from group to group. Incidents that seem incongruous to modern Americans may appear perfectly normal to Peruvian Indians. Appeals to suppressed resentment of authority may seem staid to citizens of a democracy, but uproarously funny among oppressed peoples.

"Gallows humor" provides a good example of the way social variables affect laughter. Sociologists have found many instances in which persons living under dictators have invented jokes about their tyrannical leaders—jokes that would send their authors to the gallows, were they caught. It is significant that the leader of a totalitarian state permits no open jibes. If humor had no social force, such censorship would not be necessary.

Given a different set of conditions, such humor would lose its force. There is no experimental evidence that there are national or racial differences in sense of humor. Differences appear to be cultural.

Many observers have noted that it is often impossible to translate comic effects. Few have recognized that this difficulty grows out of the fact that humor is always related to customs and ideas of a particular social climate.

A joke may be described as a wit duel between the listener and the teller. So it makes a great deal of difference who happens to be listening. Accurate analysis of Rabelais is impossible without thorough understanding of 16th-century France. And in spite of Mark Twain's place in the English-speaking world, there is no reason to believe his humor would have appealed to Chinese aristocrats of the Ming dynasty.

All these factors require us to adopt some of the attitudes of Jesus' listeners, if we hope to recognize and respond to his use of humor. It is necessary to attempt to view his sayings from the perspective of first-century Palestine rather than 20th-century America.

Any attempt to discover why Jesus used humor and how he employed it is limited not only by our tendency to view first-century situations through 20th-century eyes, but also by the traditional gravity with which the New Testament is read. We have not been moved to laughter because we have regarded the gospel message as essentially solemn— as though it were written on pages bordered in black, like Victorian funeral notices.

It is not particularly difficult, though, to recognize several cases in which Jesus, the master public speaker, seems to have employed humor for its catalytic effect upon listeners.

Modern readers tend to see nothing but the text of a sermon in the saying recorded in Matthew 11:7 (cf. Luke 7:24-25). But Jesus was speaking to herdsmen and farmers—men accustomed to outdoor life who had gone to considerable trouble to hear that strange zealot whom they called John the Baptist.

" 'What did you go out into the wilderness to behold?' " Jesus demanded. " 'A reed shaken by the wind?' "

One can almost hear him pausing for laughter before adding the jibe: " 'Why then did you go out? To see a man clothed in soft raiment?' " Obviously, a dandy was the last person one would seek in the Palestinian desert.

Again, he tells of a rich man who was a hard master. One of his servants, discharged for incompetence, makes a comment that must have provoked a roar from men accustomed to tyrannical lords: " 'What shall I do, since my master is taking away the stewardship from me? I am not strong enough to dig, and I am ashamed to beg.' " (Luke 16:1-3)

Giving a slightly different twist to the same illustrative story, just as modern after-dinner speakers vary their anecdotes in some details, Jesus has another fruitless servant tell his stonyhearted master: " 'Master, I knew you to be a hard man, reaping where you did not sow, and gathering where you did not winnow; so I was afraid, . . .' "

So far, so good. But listen to what he did:

" '. . . and I went and hid your talent in the ground. Here you have what is yours.' " (Matthew 25:24-25; cf. Luke 19:20)

That is an ancient equivalent of modern anecdotes built around a citizen's offer to pay sales tax, provided no other levy be made upon him.

Other statements appear incongruous and laugh-pro-voking when seen from the viewpoint of Jesus' actual hearers. More than once he referred to such brilliant exploits as lighting a lamp and placing it "under a bushel, or under a bed." (Mark 4:21; Luke 11:33; Luke 8:16) He asked his followers to imagine one blind man asking another blind man to guide him. (Luke 6:39)

And he told a delightfully refreshing story about the stupidity of a group of young women who went to an all-night party without sufficient oil for their lamps. That was like the modern lass who starts on a long trip without checking the gas tank of her car. Yet the foolish girls in Jesus' story had the cheek to ask their friends: " 'Give us some of your oil, for our lamps are going out.' " (Matthew 25:3-8)

One allusion must be placed in a doubtful class. It offers definite possibilities when used with a 20th-century audience. " 'I have come to set a man against his father,' " Jesus said, " 'and a daughter against her mother, *and a daughter-in-law against her mother-in-law.*' " (Matthew 10:35; [italics added]) This particular bit of incongruity may be due to modern views concerning the status of women, and may have caused no single chuckle among first-century listeners.

Even if the mother-in-law reference cannot be counted as humorous to first-century males, there remain a variety of instances in which Jesus seems to have used gross incongruity as a source of incidental humor. Far more significant in terms of both extent and emphasis are the cases in which he employed laughter as a weapon of attack.

A few persons have seen this incident as scathing sarcasm:

> "Woe to you, scribes and Pharisees, hypocrites! for you tithe mint and dill and cummin, and have neglected the weightier matters of the law, justice and mercy and faith; . . . You blind guides, straining out a gnat and swallowing a camel!"—Matthew 23:23-24 (cf. Luke 11:42)

Remember that this indictment was aired before men who probably did not tithe their hard money—and who certainly considered it ridiculous to tithe garden herbs. Camels and gnats were very much a part of their everyday life, and the superb incongruity of swallowing a camel would bring a hearty laugh whose power would be magnified because directed at tyrannical priests.

Analyzing the problem of self-criticism in religious leadership, he used language perfectly familiar to men who worked with their hands. " 'Why do you see the speck that is in your brother's eye, but do not notice the log that is in your own eye?' " As if such a ludicrous situation were not enough, he adds: " 'Or how can you say to your brother, "Brother, let me take out the speck that is in your eye," when you yourself do not see the log that is in your own eye?' " (Luke 6:41-42; cf. Matthew 7:3-4)

In this passage, humor grows out of exaggeration—a special form of incongruity. Notice, however, that this is

111

not laughter for its own sake. This is a polemic, directed against religious legalists and designed to discredit them.

Challenging hasty offers of allegiance and warning men to think before acting, Jesus told a story:

"Every one then who hears these words of mine and does them will be like a wise man who built his house upon the rock; and the rain fell, and the floods came, and the winds blew and beat upon that house, but it did not fall, because it had been founded on the rock. And every one who hears these words of mine and does not do them will be like a foolish man who built his house upon the sand; and the rain fell, and the floods came, and the winds blew and beat against that house, and it fell; and great was the fall of it."—Matthew 7:24-27

This story, whose ingredients came from the everyday lives of men who heard it, is more than a case history in which to look at Jesus' use of humor. It also indicates the role played by accumulated experience of the listener. For Luke's version of the story (Luke 6:46-49) varies from that of Matthew just as might be expected from the fact that Luke was not a native of Palestine.

Matthew is careful to specify that the foolish man built upon sand. Intimately familiar with the land, Matthew knows that many streams dry up in summer and leave sandy beds. Such spots are smooth and inviting; they tempt the novice to choose them as easy places on which to build. But after the September rains come, the sandy place will be engulfed.

No Galilean would be so foolish as to choose a dry river bed as a place to build. That idea was so utterly absurd that Jesus' choice of it as a vehicle through which to indi-

112

cate stupidity must have proved uproarous to those he addressed. If Luke didn't quite understand all details of the parable, it is small wonder that readers distant in time and space must have it explained in order to see how very funny the foolish man's house-building actually was.

Because human nature is more nearly universal than are traits of rivers, another story offers less difficulty:

> "In a certain city there was a judge who neither feared God nor regarded man; and there was a widow in that city who kept coming to him and saying, 'Vindicate me against my adversary.' For a while he refused; but afterward he said to himself, 'Though I neither fear God nor regard man, yet because this widow bothers me, I will vindicate her, or she will wear me out with her continual coming.' "—Luke 18:2-5

There is every reason to believe this story provoked broad guffaws when it was first told. Listeners knew the meaning of injustice and the indifference of judges. Here was a case in which a member of their own class outwitted authority. To make the incident completely ludicrous, the victor was that most downtrodden and helpless of all the humble—a widow. With no weapon but her tongue, she defeated one of the most powerful men in her town! Again this is humor—with a cutting edge.

Jesus mocked the religious leaders of the day for disfiguring their faces (Matthew 6:16), strutting about in pompous attire (Matthew 23:5-7), and wiping the outside of their dishes while leaving the inside dirty (Matthew 23:26, Luke 11:37). Indeed, he made fun of the Pharisees so consistently and so brilliantly that a stock literary character—the religious hypocrite—emerged under that name.

He jeered at high-placed men for acting like little children, sulking at their playmates (Matthew 11:16-19). He accused them of having trumpets blown in order to attract attention to their acts of charity (Matthew 6:2-4). And he mocked the prayer of a hard-hearted oppressor of the poor who poured the oil of adulation over his own bowed head (Luke 18:10-11).

Addressing men who had been familiar with vineyards since boyhood, he asked a question that can be only thinly veiled sarcasm: "Are grapes gathered from thorns?" he demanded, "or figs from thistles?" (Matthew 7:16; cf. Luke 11:6)

To an audience whose members regarded weddings as the gayest of all occasions, Jesus threw the mock-solemn question: " 'Can the wedding guests mourn as long as the bridegroom is with them?' " (Matthew 9:15) Note that this question was framed in answer to one suggesting that fasting in the fashion of the Pharisees was desirable.

Swinging humor like a cudgel, Jesus attacked wealth and the wealthy. He declared that " 'it is easier for a camel to go through the eye of a needle than for a rich man to enter the kingdom of God.' " (Matthew 19:23-24; cf. Mark 10:25; Luke 18:25) Prosaic scholars with a background of modern urban culture have made farfetched attempts to reduce that statement to sensible terms. Any such tampering destroys the delightful incongruity that made it laughable to those who actually heard it.

Jesus told his hearers about a rich man and a poor man. The former died and went to Hades, where he was forced to beg that the poor man come " 'dip the end of his finger in water and cool my tongue; for I am in anguish in this flame' " (Luke 16:19-24). How the exploited poor of Palestine must have chortled at such an idea!

He mocked worry over material possessions by demanding whether his hearers could add a cubit to the span of life (Matthew 6:26-29, Luke 12:25). To the modern, there is nothing inherently humorous in that question. But the oriental intimately familiar with the cubit as a unit to measure the length of a board or rope, could see the sheer absurdity of pretending to treat it as a unit of time.

On another occasion, Jesus told of a rich man whose crops were so plentiful that he had to build bigger barns; the very day they were completed, the angel of the Lord came to claim his soul (Luke 12:16-20).

He described an aristocrat who invited many to a banquet, but whose guests one after another offered ridiculous excuses. One had bought a field without looking at it, and must go examine his purchase. Another had traded for five yoke of oxen—sight unseen. And a third had just taken a wife and was in no mood for a party! (Luke 14:16-20) It is significant that the "invited guests" represented members of the opposition who refused to accept Jesus' invitation.

Even the worldly mindedness of non-Jews was mocked by Jesus. He scored "Gentiles" for being so simple-minded that they thought prayer's effectiveness measured by the volume of words used (Matthew 6:7). He ridiculed their preoccupation with material things (Matthew 6:31-32). He declared that even *they* were polite when dealing with one another (Matthew 5:45-47).

In addition to these relatively lengthy instances in which humor was a more or less prominent factor, there are dozens of cases where Jesus seems to have engaged in word play. He took delight in epigrams and near puns, used words with such invigorating freshness that nearly everything he said can be read in more than one sense. Fascinated by this quality in Jesus' speech, Gilbert K. Chesterton coined a new word and described it as *gigantesque*.

There is one indirect but suggestive bit of evidence that the gospel writers themselves were fully aware of humorous overtones in much they recorded. Mark preserves four laughter-provoking sayings, Matthew includes nineteen, and Luke records at least twenty-one. But the author of the Fourth Gospel had a special point of view to protect. Guarding his conception of the Galilean as the pre-existent *Logos*, John did not report even one saying that can be interpreted as humorous.

In terms of sheer bulk, the humor of Jesus is of more than passing importance. He employed laughter both as a device for gaining listener interest and as a weapon in his attack upon established ideas. By taking the latter course, he threw down the glove for a fight that could not end in compromise.

11

A POWERFUL STIMULUS
TO SELF-APPRAISAL

Nobody enjoys being made the object of laughter. Even the special case of the clown or professional comic is no exception. For when members of an audience respond to an entertainer by laughing, they are paying tribute to his skill rather than making fun of him as a person.

Much of the sting of the typical initiation comes from the fact that the newcomer is subjected to public humiliation. Political leaders who can shrug off attacks in newspaper editorials, often react explosively when mocked by a cartoonist. Playmates who tease a schoolboy and crook their fingers at him are inviting a fight if they do not succeed in making him cry. And in every group relationship, the person who is made the butt of a practical joke or a campaign of ridicule is likely to be prodded into some type of vigorous response.

Everybody likes to have others laugh *with* him; nobody likes to have others laugh *at* him.

Anger is one of the most frequent reactions of a person subjected to ridicule. Retaliation may take a great variety of forms, ranging from physical attack to a silent vow of revenge. But some process of striking back at those who laugh is not the only response to humiliation. A person who is mocked may react by taking a new look at himself and his goals.

Laughter is therefore among the most potent of all forces that stir men to personal re-examination. Treated in that fashion, it becomes a great awakening agent. Convicting us of failures and frailties, laughter can prod us toward new understanding of God and eagerness to accept rescue at his hand.

Old Testament prophets who disagree on many issues are at one in their insistence that God sentences whole peoples to mockery as a chastisement for sin. Hosea denounced the folly of trusting in human strength:

> Ephraim is like a dove,
>> silly and without sense,
>> calling to Egypt, going to Assyria.
>>> —Hosea 7:11

Such thinly disguised idolatry, he said, was accompanied by open turning to Baal. As a result, through the lips of the prophet God warned that

> their princes shall fall by the sword
>> because of the insolence of their tongue.
> This shall be their derision in the land of Egypt.
>>> —Hosea 7:16

Of Zedekiah and his rebellious faction, God said through Jeremiah: " 'I will make them a horror to all the kingdoms of the earth, to be a reproach, a byword, a taunt, and a curse in all the places where I shall drive them.' " (Jeremiah 24:9)

Overwhelmed by military might of Edom and other surrounding nations, Israel fell. Her ancient heights were captured and her cities laid waste. Enemies made her the subject of talk and evil gossip, gloated over her by crying, "Aha!" Her desolate fields and deserted cities became "a prey and derision to the rest of the nations round about." (Ezekiel 36:4) But it was in this prostrate state, mocked by her conquerors, that she gained capacity to hear and understand God's word in fresh fashion.

Derision was not restricted to the chosen people, however. God also caused Israel's enemies to be mocked, slapped in the face, as it were, so that military defeat and national tragedy might cause them to recognize their impotence. Few passages in literature approach the emotional level of Jeremiah's gloating over divine chastening of Moab. Reporting that God's heart moaned like a flute for these idol-worshipers, the prophet warned that calamity would reach its climax in mingled horror and derision of the chastened ones:

> "For every head is shaved and every beard cut off; upon all the hands are gashes, and on the loins is sackcloth. On all the housetops of Moab and in the squares there is nothing but lamentation; for I have broken Moab like a vessel for which no one cares, says the LORD. How it is broken! How they wail! How Moab has turned his back in shame! So Moab has become a derision and a horror to all that are round about him."—Jeremiah 48:37-39

119

Is it possible to accept such a viewpoint today? Can we concede that disaster culminating in bitter laughter of foes has any part in the scheme of providence? By any stretch of the imagination could God actually make use of derision?

Yes.

A person or a nation writhing in the agony of intense humiliation may be driven to adopt a radical new viewpoint. One who is mocked and downtrodden may, in his prostration, see life from a completely fresh perspective. For in all our activities those associated with worship and seeking for God as well as those linked with the market place, complacency and familiarity tend to make our eyes dull. In holy places as well as outside them, we have to be severely shaken if we are to see—really see—what loyalties claim our lives.

One of the high spots of a summer's religious activities at Lake Junaluska Assembly, in North Carolina, was an evening sermon by Billy Graham. It was well publicized, and keen interest was shown in advance. So on the great night, many came an hour early—fortified with pillows and reading materials.

Just before the service started, two white-haired ladies, weary with waiting, left their seats briefly. They returned to find them occupied by late comers. So the elderly saints spent the interval before the sermon in quarreling over seats from which to hear the evangelist.

Deliberately inconsistent? Not at all! They simply were not sensitive to certain aspects of their conduct. Such a state of partial slumber marks most of us most of the time. Received as a painful but growth-inducing gift from God, laughter can serve to jolt us awake.

This aspect of laughter was clearly recognized by Sören Kierkegaard. Over and over he insisted that comedy and tragedy are not wholly alien to one another. Rather, they meet at many points. As a mirror held up to life, comedy often reveals truths not reflected even by tragedy. One who is subjected to stinging laughter is challenged to recognize that he is finite. Far from being master of his fate and captain of his soul, he is confined and cribbed about. Strive as he may, he cannot save himself. If he is to escape from the human predicament, it must be through strength that is not his own.

It is here that laughter's chastening strokes can be therapeutic. All who are comfortable and spiritually assured are actually doomed; "the sons of the kingdom will be thrown into the outer darkness" (Matthew 8:12). We find no difficulty in agreeing that the gospel is "good news," but we do not always recognize that no man is eager to receive good news until he has been made sensitive by bad news.

Every great challenge—and not simply that of ridicule— leads to a state of anguish. But such anguish only intensifies the joy of creative solution. Jesus illustrated this idea from the most traumatic situation of everyday life—childbirth. "When a woman is in travail she has sorrow, because her hour has come; but when she is delivered of the child, she no longer remembers the anguish, for joy that a child is born into the world." (John 16:21)

Perhaps it would strain the idea too far to suggest that there can be no joy at all without prior anguish. But only the man who has experienced captivity can know the real meaning of release. Recognition of personal impotence is an essential prelude to victorious acceptance of divine aid. Few if any other forces equal laughter in its power to convict and condemn, making a climate in which the man who is mocked will in desperation turn to God for help.

This matter is vividly illustrated in the spiritual odyssesy of Job. Not once, but over and over, he testifies that derision has so jolted him that all his sure answers have turned into questions. His friends and associates have laughed so hard that he who once was serene, is now bewildered:

> "I am a laughingstock to my friends;
>   I, who called upon God and he answered me,
>   a just and blameless man, am a laughingstock."
>
> —Job 12:4

> "My friends scorn me;
>   my eye pours out tears to God."
>
> —Job 16:20

> "Surely there are mockers about me,
>   and my eye dwells on their provocation."
>
> —Job 17:2

Having lived for years like a chieftain or a king, Job was long sought out by other men who wanted comfort in their distress. All that has changed.

> "But now they make sport of me,
>   men who are younger than I
> whose fathers I would have disdained
>   to set with the dogs of my flock."
>
> —Job 30:1

> "And now I have become their song,
>   I am a byword to them.
> They abhor me, they keep aloof from me;
>   they do not hesitate to spit at the sight of me."
>
> —Job 30:9-10

Awakened as truly by laughter and derision as by the misfortunes that evoked mockery, Job looked about him with fresh eyes and saw a thrilling new vision of God.

In less sublime fashion, Balaam learned from laughter. It was not until he was thoroughly angry at his ass for having made sport of him that his eyes were opened to see "the angel of the LORD standing in the way, with his drawn sword in his hand." (Numbers 22:31)

Augustine credits laughter with having been the divine agent responsible for rescuing a woman from the clutches of alcohol. A maid with whom she drank called her a winebibber; startled by the insult "she looked upon her own foulness, immediately condemned it, and cast it from her." As a result, Augustine in his *Confessions* compared such a "hard and sharp taunt" with the healing scalpel used by God to cut off decayed matter at one slash.

We are prone to talk as though such spiritual decay can come "even to the best people of the church." As a matter of fact, however, it is particularly likely to afflict the good people of any community who take it for granted that they are on friendly terms with God. Gilbert and Sullivan mocked such persons as being marked by "pious platitudes and stained-glass attitudes."

Shattered by laughter, "stained-glass attitudes" can be reassembled in fresh and vigorous patterns. Just as that took place in the life of Job, so it happened repeatedly in Israel's national history. Lacking the therapeutic force of defeat and mockery, there is no assurance that the chosen people would have continued to grow in their understanding of God.

As history took shape, however, upon the fall of Jerusalem,

> the foe gloated over her,
> mocking at her downfall.

—Lamentations 1:7

Far from a casual or passing mood, this become the characteristic attitude of neighboring peoples.

> All who pass along the way
> clap their hands at you;
> they hiss and wag their heads
> at the daughter of Jerusalem.
>
> —Lamentations 2:15

Recognition that this is a fruit of sin prods the mind toward God, and consequent realization that this is his punishment.

> He drove into my heart
> the arrows of his quiver;
> I have become the laughingstock of all peoples,
> the burden of their songs all day long.
>
> —Lamentations 3:13-14

Taken into captivity and removed from the holy hill of Zion, God's people are at first desolate. Their misery is made more acute by deliberate mockery on the part of pagan overloads. Recalling this period of torment in later years, Israel's singers confessed that they wept by the waters of Babylon

> For there our captors
> required of us songs,
> and our tormenters, mirth, saying,
> "Sing us one of the songs of Zion!"
>
> —Psalm 137:3

Yet it was out of the separation, loneliness, and misery of being taunted in far-off Babylon that God's people came to recognize his presence there. No local deity whose power is limited to Canaan, God rules even in Babylon.

Over and over, seekers for God have writhed at defeat and mockery—only to emerge from torment with new passion for divine wisdom and fresh understanding of its Author. It is astonishing to scan the Psalms and recognize the degree to which they witness that both individually and socially laughter can convict in order to enlighten.

All who see me mock at me,
    they make mouths at me, they wag their heads.
But thou, O LORD, be not far off!
    O thou my help, hasten to my aid!

—Psalm 22:7, 19

. . . at my stumbling they gathered in glee,
    they gathered together against me;
cripples whom I knew not
    slandered me without ceasing;
they impiously mocked more and more,
    gnashing at me with their teeth.
Vindicate me, O LORD, my God, according to thy
      righteousness;
    and let them not rejoice over me!

—Psalm 35:15-16, 24

We have become a taunt to our neighbors,
    mocked and derided by those round about us.
Help us, O God of our salvation,
    for the glory of thy name.

—Psalm 79:4, 9

Thou hast made us the taunt of our neighbors,
    the derision and scorn of those about us.
Thou hast made us a byword among the nations,
    a laughingstock among the peoples.
Rise up, come to our help!
    Deliver us for the sake of thy steadfast love!

—Psalm 44:13-14, 26

Thou dost make us the scorn of our neighbors;
   and our enemies laugh among themselves.
Restore us, O LORD God of hosts!
   let thy face shine, that we may be saved!

—Psalm 80:6, 19

In and of itself, laughter has no spiritual power. It does not serve as an automatic prod toward God. But it can and often does awaken both individuals and peoples. Given fresh sensitivity, the mocked and convicted one is stimulated to self-appraisal and from it may turn to God with new eagerness, deeper humility. When that happens—and it can happen in the life of any who will use it as a divine corrective—laughter becomes holy.

12

SERIOUS BUSINESS, INDEED

In the lunchroom of a Midwestern department store, three young women looked up simultaneously as a woman of 65 gathered her gear to leave. She was dressed all in green, wearing an expensive suit. But her peaked hat and big bosom combined with her rough-hewn face to form a caricature of the duchess in *Alice in Wonderland*.

No doubt about it, there was something comical about her appearance and manner. So the three smartly dressed shoppers who stared at her turned to one another and exchanged broad smiles that quickly turned to giggles. At the height of their merriment, they suddenly saw that other diners had noticed their laughter and recognized its nature. So they stopped laughing and became stiffly self-conscious.

At least part of their embarrassment stemmed from recognition on the part of three fashionable ladies that their laughter was cutting. By indulging in it, they had displayed bad manners—and knew it. In the act of showing amusement at the looks of a grandmother, they convicted themselves of unkindness. So when the spotlight was turned on themselves rather than the object of their laughter, the situation became serious instead of funny.

Viewed from a God-centered perspective, much laughter is serious business, indeed. It serves to condemn those persons who are amused at the moral code, spiritual values, and messages conveyed by God's spokesmen. That is the root of the plaint in which personified Wisdom surveys the human scene and cries in the market place and at the city gates:

"How long will scoffers delight in their scoffing . . .?"
—Proverbs 1:22

Whether it be historical or legendary, Nero's joyous fiddling while Rome burned is symbolic of the deep truth here involved. For Nero is depicted as being dominated by such a set of values that he burst into ecstatic, exuberant delight as a result of tragedy. By laughing when he should have wept, he indicated his character more vividly than he could have done by any formal self-appraisal.

Along with many other analysts, Charles Darwin recognized that the line between laughter and tears is less than exact. Concerned primarily with physical reactions rather than the basic nature of emotion, he took pains to watch intently when men laughed and cried. More than once, he concluded, a person ignorant of the situation might have mistaken a late stage of amusement for grief. For

128

the naturalist saw that in some instances of violent laughter, "the tear-stained cheeks gave to the upper half of the face an expression not to be distinguished from that of a child still blubbering from grief."

On a plane far above that of attention to physical reactions from emotion, Jesus himself stressed the paradox that a given situation can produce laughter by one participant and tears by another. In a sense, we might say that two-way traffic proceeds along a highway of understanding and emotion. Those who go in one direction, laugh. But travelers along the same highway are moved to tears when proceeding in the opposite direction.

This deep problem of the human spirit is cause for both consolation and doubt. Out of it comes a promise as well as a warning.

"Blessed are you that weep now, for you shall laugh."
—Luke 6:21

But by the same token, laughter can serve to indict and to condemn:

"Woe to you that laugh now, for you shall mourn and weep."
—Luke 6:25

More is involved than a contrast between the present material life and the future spiritual life. When I laugh at the noblest and best that I encounter, I give eloquent witness to the fact that I am enslaved by ignoble goals.

Pondering the riddle of such laughter and probing the secrets of man's capacity for selective reaction to every situation he meets, the Preacher solemnly concluded

Sorrow is better than laughter,
 for by sadness of countenance the heart is made glad.

The heart of the wise is in the house of mourning;
   but the heart of fools is in the house of mirth.
It is better for a man to hear the rebuke of the wise
   than to hear the song of fools.

—Ecclesiastes 7:3-5

That is, the fool reveals himself as totally empty and vain by finding amusement in those things that should make him sad. He shows himself to be out of harmony with the values that are involved. He displays his lack of coherent understanding and sympathy with patterns of meaning.

It does not take an elaborate theological issue to illustrate the basic principle involved. In October, 1957, Lowell Thomas reported by CBS radio about recent experiences in New Guinea. Veteran traveler that he is, thoroughly aware that men of different cultures "see" events in different ways, Lowell Thomas confessed himself to be astonished.

For he had been in the audience when a group of natives from the back country saw their first motion picture. The most striking aspect of the situation, he said, was that tribesmen all laughed in the wrong places. When a character in the movie was beaten, they burst into laughter. And when someone was killed, they positively roared with delight.

Just as natives of New Guinea show they do not understand ways of Western civilization when they laugh in the wrong places of a movie, so all of us reveal our lack of sympathy with God's purposes when we make fun of the best in our culture. Such instances of laughter do not require reproof; he who laughs at the wrong things, condemns himself.

Troubled by Mordecai's independent spirit, Haman asked for advice from his wife and friends. Quite as well

130

as he, they knew Haman would be unhappy so long as God's spokesman was alive to oppose him. So they gave the prime minister a formula for a laughing good time: " 'Let a gallows fifty cubits high be made, and in the morning tell the king to have Mordecai hanged upon it; then go merrily with the king to the dinner.' " (Esther 5:14)

Much the same set of values was revealed by Ahab's emotional responses. He coveted Naboth's vineyard so strongly that he lost his appetite and was gripped in melancholy. Jezebel understood her husband completely. She devised a plot to bring about the death of Naboth by mob violence, and then urged the king to be happy: " 'Arise, and eat bread, and let your heart be cheerful; I will give you the vineyard of Naboth the Jezreelite.' " (1 Kings 21:7)

To have one's spirits revived at the prospect of another's death is so obvious an indictment that few men confess enjoyment of such a situation. But in all ages, only the sensitive ones who are attuned to God's voice recognize that much horseplay and mockery is deadly serious. Out of such concern for taking serious things seriously come two of the most fearful warnings of the Old Testament:

He who mocks the poor insults his Maker;
  he who is glad at calamity will not go unpunished.

—Proverbs 17:5

The eye that mocks a father
  and scorns to obey a mother
will be picked out by the ravens of the valley
  and eaten by the vultures.

—Proverbs 30:17

If it is a source of condemnation to make fun of parental controls and to laugh at the misfortunes of other men,

131

ridicule of a divine messenger should be a cause for horror. Recognition of this fundamental principle is the key to deep meanings in one of the most enigmatic stories of Scripture.

Focus upon the bare details of Elisha's encounters with mocking boys will lead to bewilderment, if not outright rejection of the story. But taken as a vehicle through which to seek the meaning of laughter at a spokesman for God, the story emerges as luminous.

Elijah's spirit descended upon Elisha and he performed various mighty works to prove, beyond dispute, that he was an authentic representative of God. In that role he stood in sharp contrast to the "sons of the prophet" who had social status but little spiritual discernment. After demonstrating his own power by showing himself superior to spokesmen for official religion—and therefore the genuine messenger of the Lord—Elisha went up from Jericho to Bethel.

> . . . and while he was going up on the way, some small boys came out of the city and jeered at him, saying, "Go up, you baldhead! Go up, you baldhead!" And he turned around, and when he saw them, he cursed them in the name of the LORD. And two she-bears came out of the woods and tore forty-two of the boys.—2 Kings 2:23-24

Some symbolism of that story is probably lost forever. Just what was suggested by the baldhead jibe and the number forty-two, it is impossible to surmise. But whatever else that story may suggest, it certainly does communicate a deep truth about laughter. When persons who are "small boys" in their understanding of God and his ways break into merriment upon meeting a genuine representative of the Most High, fearful consequences are certain to follow.

132

Their jeers cause tragedy to break upon their own heads.

Authentic word from God is always likely to be "a torment to those who dwell on the earth" (Revelation 11:10). It is so challenging, so disturbing, so disruptive of the taken-for-granted, so troubling to the complacent soul that rejection and laughter are natural responses. It is a commonplace that prophets are likely to suffer not only physical attack, but also mockery (Ezekiel 21:10, Hebrews 11:36).

Such reactions by men incapable of assimilating the word of God are so common that a pattern of warning followed by mockery is likely to occur over and over until disaster comes. That was the case in the evil reign of Zedekiah, followed by leading priests and the people in his rebellion against God.

> The LORD, the God of their fathers, sent persistently to them by his messengers, because he had compassion on his people and on his dwelling place; but they kept mocking the messengers of God, despising his words, and scoffing at his prophets, till the wrath of the LORD rose against his people, till there was no remedy.—2 Chronicles 36:15-16

It is surprising that a matter so fundamental in human thought and action has received so little formal attention. Western civilization has tended to magnify the value of laughter, without inquiring about its many varieties or falling back in dread at those kinds of merrymaking that provoke divine wrath.

Our survey has already indicated that prophets, poets, and seers of Israel took this matter very seriously, indeed. Without producing formal analyses of it, inspired messengers of God studded their works with brief comments indicating the dangers in laughter that condemns those who engage in it.

Isaiah took it as a basic principle that scornful laughter brings its own punishment; "the ruthless shall come to nought and the scoffer cease." (Isaiah 29:20) But he knew quite well that his own prophetic announcement of divine wrath would evoke ridicule. Almost in one breath, as it were, he urged men not to add to their troubles by scoffing and simultaneously insisted that national woes were at hand:

> Now therefore do not scoff,
>> lest your bonds be made strong;
> for I have heard a decree of destruction
>> from the Lord God of hosts upon the whole land.
>
> —Isaiah 28:22

Folk wisdom, incorporated in capsule sayings of the Proverbs, suggested that

>> Even in laughter the heart is sad,
>>> and the end of joy is grief.
>>
>> —Proverbs 14:13

Simultaneously, it urged all men to remember that
>> Condemnation is ready for scoffers,
>>> and flogging for the backs of fools.
>>
>> —Proverbs 19:29

In spite of such guides to thought and conduct, it has always been evident that only a minority will give heed. It is the way of least resistance to revile, make fun, and ridicule that which is higher and better than one practices. Consequently, Jude reports that even the love feasts of the early church were marred by carousal. That will be true so long as men are men; " 'In the last time there will be scoffers, following their own ungodly passions.' " (Jude, verse 18)

To laugh for the sake of making a noise, to make fun of the noble and holy, is perhaps the most subtle of all man's ways of rejecting the appeal of God. Precisely to the degree that such activity seems hilarious, it is actually serious. Laughter can function as an indictment fashioned by the man who laughs.

13

LET EVERY MAN REJOICE
THAT HE IS A MAN!

Pondering the ways of God and of men, Israel's seers were continually overwhelmed by the creative thread that runs through the universe. Unable to communicate their awe except in figurative terms, they personified the divine creative force and spoke of it as Wisdom.

Wisdom is both the subject of man's striving and his companion on the pilgrimage that leads to it. Wisdom condemns, challenges, prods—and delights. Much of the Book of Proverbs is devoted to capsule commentaries about Wisdom, and to insights gained through courtship of Wisdom.

As described in poetic oriental language of Proverbs,

Wisdom was formed by God before the work of creation in order to be his aide in the making of the world. Wisdom took part in the building of the heavens and the vaulting of the waters. Wisdom was present when the sea was enclosed, and took part in laying the foundations of the world. But it was when God made men that Wisdom came into her own and found her real reason to be. In the translation of Ronald Knox, Wisdom's autobiography witnesses: "I was at his side, a master-workman, my delight increasing with each day, as I made play before him all the while; made play in this world of dust, with the sons of Adam for my playfellows." (Proverbs 8:30-31)[1]

What a queer idea!

Reverence for God's creative power, of which man partakes, is indicated in a formula that makes the word of creation display the qualities of play. Can it be that there is something delightful, even laughable, about discovery, outreach, and exercise of creative potential?

More than one cultural group far from Canaan has shared this viewpoint with the chosen people. South Australian mythology includes a creation story in which man is molded, then tickled so that the creature shaped in the image of deity is caused to laugh and come to life.

Tribesmen of the Central Celebes have rituals that require men to pose riddles after their rice is planted. Laughter at solution of a riddle is followed by solemn intonation of the formula: "Let our rice come up, let fat ears come up both in the lowlands and on the heights." Anthropologists who studied that strange custom concluded that laughter is deliberately invoked at the planting season, because it is believed to have power to bring new life into being.

---

[1]From the *Old Testament,* Vol. II, in the translation of Monsignor Ronald Knox, Copyright 1950, Sheed and Ward, Inc., New York. Used by permission.

According to an ancient legend preserved in New South Wales, fire (one of man's chief tools in his own creative re-shaping of the world) was originally owned by two women. Kangaroo Rat and Bronze-winged Pigeon knew that fire was the key to godlike power, so kept their treasure concealed in a nut shell.

Other animals finally discovered how these two women cooked their food, so they devised a plot. Owners of the fire were invited to a dance, at which one animal after another gave a comical performance. At last the two guests could control themselves no longer. Engulfed with merriment, they laughed aloud and rolled on the ground. Conspirators seized the nut, opened it, and set fire among the trees—from whence it has been available ever since, by friction.

Laughter linked with the marvel of creativity also appears in the Australian myth of Gourgourgahgah. This bird—whose name seems to imitate the sounds of convulsive merriment—was given just one task by the gods. Each dawn as the morning star pales, Gourgourgahgah laughs in order to cause the day to break. Out of the death of night, there comes the life of day—signaled by laughter.

Primitive as it seems at first look, such a view is not altogether foreign to New Testament emphases. Out of the symbolic return home of the lost son, there came spontaneous joyful feasting. Challenged by the elder brother, such a reaction was defended and interpreted by the father: " ' "It was fitting to make merry and be glad, for this your brother was dead, and is alive; he was lost, and is found." ' " (Luke 15:32)

Set in a quite different context, the same point of view is reflected in Jesus' analysis of the paradoxical changes that will accompany the coming of the new spiritual age.

"When a woman is in travail she has sorrow, because her hour has come; but when she is delivered of the child, she no longer remembers the anguish, for joy that a child is born into the world. So you have sorrow now, but I will see you again and your hearts will rejoice, and no one will take your joy from you. On that day you will ask me no questions."—John 16:21-22

So viewed, joy and laughter are natural and spontaneous aspects of participating in or recognizing the creative work of God. That being the case, it would seem that Scripture and literature would preserve case histories in which men have made merry in order feebly to communicate their praise of the Creator.

That is precisely what happened in the climactic moment of Israel's history that saw the ark of the covenant brought to Jerusalem. Carried on a new cart, the sacred symbol of the presence of the Most High was the central object of a great procession. But instead of being sedate, the occasion was marked by exercises that on the surface were indistinguishable from secular festivities: "And David and all the house of Israel were making merry before the LORD with all their might, with songs and lyres and harps and tambourines and castanets and cymbals." (2 Samuel 6:5)

It is not strange that Michal the daughter of Saul should have reacted by scolding her husband for his leaping and dancing. He made a shameless exhibition of himself, she said, and what might he have to say in his defense?

David replied by reminding his wife that he danced not for the benefit of human spectators, but "before the LORD." That is, his making merry was a form of praise. Through the vehicle of dancing and laughing, he indicated praise too profound to be expressed in more sober style.

That is the theme of the famous thirteenth-century

legend, "The Tumbler of Our Lady." Retold many times, it is perhaps best known under the title, "The Juggler of Notre Dame."

Early versions of the tumber's tale circulated in Latin and may have been familiar before the First Crusade. A wandering tumbler, having become a novice in the Cistercian order, finds himself unable to follow the complexities of ritualistic worship. He does not wish to be considered indifferent, so in desperation he slips into an obscure crypt and performs the only office he knows—that of juggling. He is fearful of offending God, but is unable to express his veneration in any other fashion. So at every hour of prayer he tumbles before a little altar.

Observed by his brethren and censured, he dies during a dance of praise and his spirit is received in heaven by hosts of angels and archangels. Lacking experience and skill with which to communicate his praise through words and ritualistic acts, the tumbler used the only medium of which he was master. Therefore, though his tumbling had surface parallels with that designed purely to entertain a crowd, it was an act of deepest worship.

Such was the case with David's making merry and dancing before the ark. Through a medium chiefly used to express delight of lower types, David laughed in order to indicate his ineffable joy at the presence of the Lord GOD of hosts, maker of the heavens and the earth and all they contain.

Some who have pondered the riddle of laughter have regarded it as being heard in purest form when it comes as a result of being involved in the creative process. According to this view, delight is a natural product of discovery and outreach. Delight, in turn, is signaled by laughter.

Whatever else may be said for it, this view is intriguing. For it offers fresh clues as to why man is the only creature who laughs. Made in the image of God—that is, endowed with capacity to engage in the creative process—alone among earth's inhabitants, man has power to invent, discover, create, imagine, and conceive. Since no bird or animal can think a new thought or paint an original picture or come in fear and trembling into fresh encounter with God, these creatures cannot experience the delight of discovery. Therefore they have no capacity to develop a response such as laughter.

Our survey of laughter in the Bible has already suggested that no one theory or interpretation is big enough to include all instances of this most human of activities. But the fact that much laughter is neither an effect of creative discovery nor a vehicle through which to praise the Creator does not mean that the theory has no merit.

Approaching the matter from the viewpoint of philosophy rather than theology, Aristotle concluded that men value art because it is part of our nature to enjoy learning. All viewing of artistic works, he suggested, involves an act of "recognizing" what is depicted. That is, the viewer follows in the footsteps of the originator and rediscovers what the painter saw and depicted. This creative outreach is a kind of learning, and consequently brings pleasure. When such pleasure comes quickly on a large scale, it has the effect of producing laughter.

Aristotle developed his theory from analysis of human reactions to the work of painters. But his view is equally pertinent in relation to any field of creative discovery: music, sculpture, literature, the dance, religious ritual, and even scientific invention. Autobiographies of great scientists are studded with references to the "unspeakable joy" that floods a man's soul when he is overwhelmed by a discovery in mathematics or physics or astronomy.

On a much lower level, something of the same effect may follow the sudden mastering of an opponent in table tennis, solving a jigsaw puzzle, or coming to understand a theorem

141

in tenth-grade geometry. Addison called such effects "the pleasure of the imagination." In less sophisticated and more universal form, it may be that this idea of delight in accomplishing new things and doing the unexpected is at the heart of such stories as that of Aladdin and his magic lamp.

Since encounter with God and deepened understanding of his ways is the most sublime of creative experiences, it follows that joy should be a primary by-product of the religious quest. Laughter of personal enlargement should be more frequent than laughter of amusement—though the casual listener might be unable to distinguish between the two.

Psalm 1 is much more than an introduction to the psalter. It sets a major keynote of this most sublime of devotional anthologies when it insists that blessedness is linked with finding *delight* in the law of the LORD. Far from being merely a stern discipline, the quest for God and his ways is a joyously glad pilgrimage on which each new day reveals fresh vistas. Each fresh discovery of truth sheds its own radiance;

> Thy testimonies are my delight,
> they are my counselors.
> —Psalm 119:24

Long ago, Jeremy Taylor pointed out that man's capacity to be a man—that is, to exercise his creative power and make real the image of God that is latent in him—comes to its apex in the hope for life eternal. Joy that stems from coming into meeting with this hope is sufficient to make a man victor over any disaster life can bring. It is in this sense that Israel's prophets and psalmists testify so powerfully to the pleasure of finding refuge in God.

> . . . let all who take refuge in thee rejoice,
> let them ever sing for joy;

and do thou defend them,
 that those who love thy name may exult in thee.
—Psalm 5:11

Prodding Job into a re-examination of his system of values, Bildad the Shuhite promises that if Job is indeed blameless, God will receive and shelter him.

 "He will yet fill your mouth with laughter,
  and your lips with shouting."
—Job 8:21

Recognition of such an emphasis is not to suggest that the creative divine-human encounter, which gives meaning and direction to human life, is amusing in any light sense of the word. Confronted with the mystery in which the Savior demonstrated God's power to bring life out of death, Mary Magdalene and the women were simultaneously overpowered with "fear and great joy" (Matthew 28:8).

That man who has met God, and who therefore rejoices that he is a man made in the image of God, may break into laughter that to the dull of spirit sounds strangely like echoes of madness. For the element of conscious dread that marks a meeting with God gives new qualities to the delight that it accompanies.

It is the witness of the centuries that the most fundamental need of man is Someone with whom he can be *at one*. That is the heart of Augustine's famous cry: "Thou has made us for Thyself, O God, and our hearts are restless until they find their rest in Thee."

It is an enigma that the only perfect freedom is found in captivity to God. Much the same reconciliation of opposites is involved in the delight that comes from creative surrender that at one and the same time makes man conscious of his creaturehood, and radiantly aware of the divine spark within him. Augustine expressed this idea for all time in his *Confessions*.

Far be it, O Lord, far be it from the heart of Thy servant who is confessing to Thee, far be it that I should consider myself happy by virtue of just any joy which I experience. For, there is a joy which is not given to the wicked; but rather to them who serve Thee for Thine own sake; for such people, Thou Thyself art joy. And this is the happy life, to rejoice unto Thee, from Thee, on account of Thee: this it is and there is none other.

Joyful "gospel songs" that do not quite achieve the dignity of hymns sometimes succeed in expressing the delight that stems from even a brief moment in God's transforming presence. Such moments are in Peter's mind as he exhorts men to repent "that times of refreshing may come from the presence of the Lord" (Acts 3:19). This is the joy of the camp meeting at its best, the joy of the life-changing conversion, the joy of solitary encounter with God that leaves one so ecstatic he has no words with which to tell men of his hour on Sinai.

It is not simply a slogan or a party cry or an inherited verbal formula by which the gospel is equated with an invitation to delight from creative enlargement of the self. Good news is the heart of Christianity.

"Thanks be to God through Jesus Christ our Lord!" (Romans 7:25) I have been so fashioned that I have capacity to meet God and be remade through that meeting. Therefore with Paul who once was Saul, not in spite of the fact that I am perpetually in fear and trembling but because of it, I need to shout: "Rejoice!" (Philippians 1:18; 1 Thessalonians 5:16; Romans 15:10; Galatians 4:27)

Laugh in the face of adversity and disaster. Find delight in searching out the law of the Lord. Exercise your God-given capacity for enlargement of mind and soul, finding joy too exalted for words. "Rejoice in the Lord always; again I will say, Rejoice" (Philippians 4:4).

14

A TOKEN OF VICTORY

"Mrs. Victor Richards would appreciate a call. She's a devoted member of First Church, 82 years old, whose daughter died last week."

To the new pastor of an eastern church, the memorandum seemed routine. Here was a lonely soul who needed solace; at the first opportunity, he would go and try to cheer her.

That opportunity did not come until late on Thursday afternoon. As he knocked at the door of the cheap frame house, the minister grimaced at the prospect of squalor and melancholy to be encountered. But his mood quickly altered. Hobbling to the door as rapidly as her old legs permitted, the stranger introduced herself as Mother Viola.

As they talked about the death of her daughter, she positively beamed. "I should be sad, but I'm not," she said. "Effie was a good woman, and I'm sure she's gone to heaven. I ought to be lonely, but I can't. God is here with me, watching over me, and I feel his presence every hour. I've tried to serve him since I was ten, and in all these seventy-two years he hasn't let me down—not once!"

An observer at a distance would have thought that Mother Viola laughed aloud several times during the conversation. A bright smile played over her benign face, and her voice was gay. Though she did not actually break out in laughter of merriment, her whole manner showed that she found delight in life. She smiled as a token of victory, rejoicing that through God she had found strength to conquer poverty, loneliness, old age, and death.

Gentle laughter of that sort is far removed from the titters evoked by a funny story or the guffaws that stem from antics of a clown. It is not so much a reaction to a specific situation as it is a pervasive mood of exalted joy. Those who come into meeting with it from a viewpoint other than interest in laughter, might even describe it as "peace of soul" or "victorious faith."

That such a state of confident bliss actually does deserve consideration in a survey of laughter is indicated by the prayer of Psalm 90:

> Satisfy us in the morning with thy steadfast love,
>   that we may rejoice and be glad all our days.
> Make us glad as many days as thou has afflicted us,
>   and as many years as we have seen evil.
>
> —Psalm 90:14-15

Many spiritual giants have concurred in saying that one

cannot become saintly by retreating from life. Sanctity stems, instead, from meeting life head-on and by the grace of God overcoming illness, disappointment, heartache, and defeat. Peace of soul does not result from living without tension, but is a fruit of victory over those tensions that will break any man who tries to meet them in his own strength. That refreshment which is promised in the great invitation of Jesus is a product of striving.

Just as the strength of God comes to the seeker after God, so gladness flows as a result of recognizing the protection of our divine Champion.

> Clap your hands, all peoples!
> Shout to God with loud songs of joy!
> For the LORD, the Most High, is terrible,
> a great king over all the earth.
> —Psalm 47:1-2

Any woes that may come are transient and insignificant, linked with a brief earthly sojourn and subject to radical change in the coming spiritual realm. "In the world you have tribulation," Jesus pointed out; "but be of good cheer, I have overcome the world" (John 16:33).

Confident trust in the victory won by Christ and made available to his own is a source of sublime happiness not simply in heaven, but here and now. "Though you do not now see him you believe in him and rejoice with unutterable and exalted joy" (1 Peter 1:8).

That mood is not a fruit of shelter of such nature that it eliminates stress. Always, those who seek after righteousness are targets for plots of evil men. In every age, there is some powerful oppressor whose razor tongue and treacherous mind is bent upon taking advantage of the innocent. No matter what the burdens created by such a situation, God will eventually bring relief by uprooting the mighty one. When that happens,

147

The righteous shall see, and fear,
   and shall laugh at him, saying,
"See the man who would not make God his refuge,
   but trusted in the abundance of his riches,
      and sought refuge in his wealth!"

—Psalm 52:6-7

Besides such witness to general deliverance at the divine hand, Scripture preserves vivid testimonials to specific instances of national and individual rescue. Given divine strength in order to rebound from despair, a sweet singer of Israel rejoices:

Thou hast turned for me my mourning into dancing;
   thou hast loosed my sackcloth
   and girded me with gladness,
that my soul may praise thee and not be silent.
   O LORD my God, I will give thanks to thee for ever.

—Psalm 30:11-12

Remembering some great national deliverance—perhaps the return from Babylonian captivity—God's people testified that

When the LORD restored the fortunes of Zion,
   we were like those who dream.
Then our mouth was filled with laughter,
   and our tongue with shouts of joy.

—Psalm 126:1-2

Just such a reaction came from a man lame from birth, made whole through being blessed by Peter. On gaining strength as a gift from God through Christ, he reacted extravagantly; "leaping up he stood and walked and entered the temple with them, walking and leaping and praising God" (Acts 3:8). Instead of having a crippled

148

body set free, the Ethiopian eunuch was spiritually emancipated by Philip's summary of the good news of Jesus—and "went on his way rejoicing" (Acts 8:39).

God's continual rescue, vividly recognized, is a source of continuous delight so profound that it can be expressed only through worship.

> Let us come into his presence with thanksgiving;
>> let us make a joyful noise to him with songs of praise!
>> —Psalm 95:2

In such a mood, let the rescued one cast dignity to the winds. Some who hear will criticize, and others will fail to understand. Never mind; break out in glad witness to God's redemptive power. "Is any cheerful? Let him sing praise" (James 5:13). Too often, we restrain our joy and make worship artificially solemn.

A partial corrective consists in giving due attention both to the nature of joy and special occasions for demonstrating it. The Feast of Purim, still observed by orthodox Jews, might be called "a ceremony of laughter." On Purim eve, even the synagogue is a place of merriment. Celebrating divine deliverance in general, and the victory of Mordecai over Haman in particular, "therefore do the Jews make the fourteenth day of the month of Adar a day of gladness."

That such a festival is not alien to the spirit of faith, but an integral part of it, is indicated by Isaiah's great vision. God's reign and his perpetual redirection of human affairs, constitutes a glad motif:

> "Hark, your watchmen lift up their voice,
>> together they sing for joy;
> for eye to eye they see
>> the return of the LORD to Zion.
> Break forth together into singing,
>> you waste places of Jerusalem;

149

for the LORD has comforted his people,
    he has redeemed Jerusalem."
                                        —Isaiah 52:8-9

Much the same emphasis is symbolized in the character-istic title of the Christian faith: "Gospel." Christ and his message literally constitute "good news"; gaiety and joy and laughter at their highest and best come to focus, as it were, in a system so gloriously wonderful that it can only be called *the gospel.* "These things have I spoken to you, that my joy may be in you, and that your joy may be full" (John 15:11).

Long before God's self-disclosure and process of sheltering came to finality in Christ, the people of the covenant dis-covered many secrets of joyful living. It stems from a set of values and a life goal shaped by unqualified allegiance to God, said many an early seer. Eliphaz spoke bluntly when he rebuked Job for linking material prosperity and tranquility with a God-guided life of happiness:

"Behold, happy is the man whom God reproves;
    therefore despise not the chastening of the Almighty.
For he wounds, but he binds up;
    he smites, but his hands heal."
                                        —Job 5:17-18

That this is no merely symbolic, but a very practical promise, is indicated by the triumphant life of Paul. Speak-ing for all conscious of having peace with God, he exulted that "we rejoice in our hope of sharing the glory of God. More than that, we rejoice in our sufferings . . . " (Romans 5:2-3).

Once that point of view is accepted, it is possible to pro-ceed to the joyful and triumphant declaration that defeat is not an alternative:

At destruction and famine you shall laugh . . .
                                        —Job 5:22

Capacity to laugh at destruction and famine stems from allegiance to a set of values according to which the significant things of life are spiritual, not material. Consequently, such laughter—specified or implied in the life of most great men of God—signifies victory. Forces that once threatened have been overcome and may be dismissed as harmless. Fears that dominate the natural man have vanished in the radiant light of God's abiding presence. Doubts that made the long night hours miserable have been banished altogether.

Triumphant at having gained such a victory, it is natural to be merry and gay. A kindergarten child, chased by an older playmate, laughs upon reaching the security of his mother's arms. Just so, the consciously protected child of God will spontaneously erupt into glad praise.

... Thus says the LORD God:
   ... behold, my servants shall sing for gladness of heart"
              —Isaiah 65:13, 14

Evil and rebellious men will fall under the weight of their own guilt,

   But let all who take refuge in thee rejoice,
      let them ever sing for joy;
   and do thou defend them,
      that those who love thy name may exult in thee.
              —Psalm 5:11

Because glad exultation is an inevitable by-product of finding delight in the quest for the kingdom, men fall into two distinct categories.

   All the days of the afflicted are evil,
      but a cheerful heart has a continual feast.
              —Proverbs 15:15

Paradoxical as it seems, such gaiety comes to God's own not in spite of a life context that includes struggle, but actually because of it.

> "Blessed are you when men revile you and persecute you and utter all kinds of evil against you falsely on my account. Rejoice and be glad, for your reward is great in heaven, for so men persecuted the prophets who were before you."
> —Matthew 5:11

Radiant ones of the early church, still deliriously happy at the incredible gift of God's own Son for rescue of men, took the promise of joy as a literal one—and therefore made it effective in their lives. Arrested, beaten, and threatened, apostles could scarcely restrain their feet from dancing as they walked out of the council, "rejoicing that they were counted worthy to suffer dishonor for the name" (Acts 5:41). Persecuted and driven out of their missionary field because devout women and leading men turned against them, Paul and Barnabas were in utter defeat. Simultaneously, however, they were "filled with joy and the Holy Spirit" (Acts 13:52).

Joy in defeat . . . gladness in persecution . . . laughter at destruction and famine . . . singing under divine chastening. . . .

Laughter that symbolizes victory over stress and challenge is of many types. It may be manifested by outward signs ranging from an exuberant shout to a quiet smile. It may come as a result of sudden rescue from danger or as an effect of slow growth in understanding of God's way. Whatever its nature and however it is indicated, such triumphant joy is likely to be paradoxical—no pure state of unmixed delight, but a sense of victory in the midst of continuing attack. True servants of God through Christ are likely, with Paul and his fellow workers, to feel that simultaneously they

> are treated as imposters, and yet are true; as
> unknown, and yet well known; as dying, and be-
> hold we live; as punished, and yet not killed; as
> sorrowful, yet always rejoicing; as poor, yet mak-
> ing many rich; as having nothing, and yet pos-
> sessing everything.—2 Corinthians 6:8-10

Achieved in that fashion, joy is sublime. Pursuit of it is a wholly worthy activity, so self-rewarding that it is fitting for a saint to exhort each of us to engage in it: "Never flag in zeal, be aglow with the Spirit, serve the Lord. Rejoice in your hope, be patient in tribulation . . . " (Romans 12:11-12).

Interpreted in this fashion, "laughter" in its broadest sense is a gift so exalted that it can be the subject of a fervent benediction eagerly sought by an apostle for his fellows in all ages: "May the God of hope fill you with all joy and peace in believing" (Romans 15:13).

15

THE LAUGHTER OF GOD

Joy is universally associated with religion at its best. Inescapably, almost inevitably, the symbols of heaven and of spiritual reward stress the notion of endless bliss.

So it is taken for granted that God experiences delight. Most readers of the New Testament accept without difficulty the idea that it gives God pleasure to have his children enter into right relationship with him. Indeed, the three parables of Luke, chapter 15 are among the best loved of the Gospel record, and each stresses the Father's experience of joy.

" ' . . . there will be more joy in heaven over one sinner who repents than over ninety-nine righteous

154

persons who need no repentance.

" ' . . . there is joy before the angels of God over one sinner who repents.

" ' . . . It was fitting to make merry and be glad, for this your brother was dead, and is alive; he was lost, and is found.' "

—Luke 15:7, 10, 32

Still another position in the spectrum of laughter is readily and widely attributed to God. That he scorns the pretensions and achievements of men, we grant without hesitation.

> He scorns the tumult of the city;
>   he hears not the shouts of the driver.
>
> —Job 39:7

> Toward the scorners he is scornful,
>   but to the humble he shows favor.
>
> —Proverbs 3:34

> God scorns the wicked,
>   but the upright enjoy his favor.
>
> —Proverbs 14:9

Traditional thought accepts so much, without balking. But can it be that God actually laughs? Do we commit blasphemy by so much as suggesting that the Maker of the heavens and the earth might be amused?

This question has engaged the attention of several commentators upon the Psalms, who confess themselves puzzled by references there. Because many devout persons react negatively to suggestions that God actually does laugh, it has been suggested that we have a basic distrust for the very process of laughing. Again, it has been charged that dour and solemn seekers after God have attributed their own melancholy to him.

155

What is the biblical position?

According to prophets and poets in the period when Israel's awareness of God was in its greatest flower, it is not simply proper but actually necessary for us to recognize that God does laugh. For as Scripture interprets divine laughter, it is a challenge and a corrective directed against the follies, pretensions, and rebellions of men.

Such a reaction on the part of God is evoked by both individuals and nations. Heard by sensitive ones who listen for every tiny whisper from the lips of God, mocking laughter from heaven strikes fear into the heart. In its basic function, therefore, the laughter of God is a warning and a corrective. It reminds us that we are men and not gods. It warns us that all our achievements are finite. It stirs us to recognize that those things we consider most stable and enduring, those men and institutions we regard as most powerful, are actually subject to ridicule.

That proud and haughty one who rides roughshod over the meek, should evoke laughter instead of fierce resentment. In the sight of God, he is simply a seven-day locust whose very memory will be forgotten before one instant of eternity has passed.

> Yet a little while, and the wicked will be no more;
>> though you look well at his place, he will not be there.
> The wicked plots against the righteous,
>> and gnashes his teeth at him;
> but the LORD laughs at the wicked,
>> for he sees that his day is coming.

—Psalm 37: 10, 12-13

Wisdom, personified as interpreter of divine secrets, gives every man a chance. She is vociferous in crying out her challenges, but blunt in her warning to those who close their ears:

Because I have called and you refused to listen,
I also will laugh at your calamity;
I will mock when panic strikes you.

—Proverbs 1:24, 26

As with men, so with nations. Those who defy the Lord may prosper temporarily. To the dull of hearing, it may seem that boasts of kings and generals are the loudest of all noises. But sensitive ones hear above their shouts and threats the sardonic laughter of God.

The kings of the earth set themselves,
and the rulers take counsel together,
against the LORD and his anointed . . .
He who sits in the heavens laughs;
the LORD has them in derision.

—Psalm 2:2-4

Treacherous and bloodthirsty men who lead the fighting forces of evil nations prowl 'round and 'round God's own, snarling like dogs and thinking they will not be heard in heaven.

But thou, O LORD, dost laugh at them;
thou dost hold all the nations in derision.

—Psalm 59:8

Though neither "laughter" nor its synonyms occur in the passage, the most magnificent of all biblical lines depicting God's mockery of the pretensions of men is preserved in the history of the kings of Israel. Appropriately, it is linked with the fame and exploits of that mightiest of stalwarts, Sennacherib. Begging Hezekiah to lift his eyes above the earth and center upon abiding things, Isaiah reported that God told him how "the daughter of Jerusalem" despised, scorned, and wagged her head at the king of Assyria.

157

Such utterly undiplomatic language must have been designed to shock Hezekiah. But it was simply a prelude to the description of the way God will make sport of the most powerful man on earth. Speaking to the conqueror through Isaiah, God thunders:

> "Because you have raged against me
>   and your arrogance has come into my ears,
> I will put my hook in your nose
>   and my bit in your mouth,
> and I will turn you back on the way
>   by which you came."
>
> —2 Kings 19:28; Isaiah 37:29

Of course, such judgment does not necessarily come in the way men expect or at a time they think appropriate. A thousand years in God's sight are but as yesterday; he may withhold his laughter so long that men grow weary of waiting and wonder if he has turned aside. Moab struts and preens among the nations, fierce in his strength and fearful in treatment of the defeated. But in the end little Israel, whose strength comes from God, makes mockery of the mighty one "so that Moab shall wallow in his vomit, and he too shall be held in derision" (Jeremiah 48:26).

Make no mistake about it. Any point of view according to which God laughs, raises difficulties. Overwhelmed by troubles and so vehement in protesting innocence that he will not listen to charges of friends, Job lashes out at God and accuses him of moral indifference:

> It is all one; therefore I say,
>   he destroys both the blameless and the wicked.
> When disaster brings sudden death,
>   he mocks at the calamity of the innocent.
>
> —Job 9:22

Wrestling with the problem of why the good die young and the evil flourish to hearty old age, the writer of the apocryphal Book of Wisdom insists that things are not as they seem at first look. God will have his laugh sooner or later. Wicked men are contemptuous of God because those who seek him suffer and die. "And they themselves, all the while, are earning the Lord's contempt; they themselves, doomed to lie there dishonoured among the dead, eternally a laughing-stock!" (Book of Wisdom, 4:18)[1]

Pondering this matter in *The Justification of God,* P. T. Forsyth was forced to reckon with the apparent delay in God's working of his will. "There is a judgment," he concluded, "which is not visitation but irony. Its tarrying works upon us more than its coming. . . . If God does not yet intervene on earth He sits in heaven—sits and laughs. . . . The heavens are not so simple as they seem, nor is God so mocked as He consents to appear, and to appear for long."

That is, God always has the last laugh. It may be delayed; evil may appear to have conquered. But in the end, God prevails.

To ask for easy answers is to beg the question. There is a gulf between the human and the divine, and no bridge of fixed and final understanding can be thrown across it. "No one has ever seen God" (John 1:18). His ways are "past finding out." His judgment is "unsearchable."

Echoing the verdict of Scripture, *The Imitation of Christ* insists upon God's capacity to accomplish things no man can understand. "If the works of God were such that they might be easily comprehended by human reason, they could not justly be called marvellous or unspeakable."

Without pretending or even seeking fully to understand it, we can therefore accept the biblical view that God

---

[1] *Op. cit.*

159

actually does laugh. Like the creature made in his image, the Creator engages in this most characteristic and mysterious of creative responses. He mocks the pretensions of men in order to strike fear into our hearts and cause us to think of him instead of finite things. He scorns the boasting of the wicked, knowing that the apparent triumph of evil is temporary and illusory.

So far, detailed analyses of inspired writers take us. Yet this is not the end. Suggestive and sublime as is the divine mockery of man's futile attempts at rebellion, it is not the last sound that echoes from the lips of the Creator.

Though it is nowhere specified, it is everywhere implied in scripture that God also laughs with pure delight at bringing his own unto himself. This is the final and definitive form of laughter—a cosmic witness to the dignity and enduringness of the soul of the creature made a little lower than the angels, whose capacity to laugh symbolizes that he is in very truth restless until he finds his rest in God.